～ *Angela Hutchinson Hammer*

*Betty Hammer Joy*

# ANGELA

# HUTCHINSON

# HAMMER

⁓ Arizona's Pioneer Newspaperwoman

BETTY E. HAMMER JOY

The University of Arizona Press

*Tucson*

The University of Arizona Press
© 2005 The Arizona Board of Regents
All rights reserved
♾ This book is printed on acid-free, archival-quality paper.
Manufactured in the United States of America

10   09   08   07   06   05      6   5   4   3   2   1

Library of Congress Cataloging-in-Publication Data
Joy, Betty E. Hammer (Betty Evangeline Hammer), 1932–
Angela Hutchinson Hammer : Arizona's pioneer
newspaperwoman / Betty E. Hammer Joy.
p. cm.
Includes bibliographical references and index.
ISBN-13: 978-0-8165-2357-3 (pbk. : alk. paper)
ISBN-10: 0-8165-2357-6 (pbk. : alk. paper)
1. Hammer, Angela Hutchinson, 1870–1952. 2. Journalists—
United States—Biography. 3. Journalists—Arizona—Biography.
4. Women journalists—United States—Biography. 5. Women
journalists—Arizona—Biography. I. Title.
PN4874.H2237J68 2005
070.4'3'092—dc22

                              2005004939

To Chris, Anna, Marilyn, Cy, Rebecca, my grandchildren,

and to all the progeny of the Hutchinson sisters as you each

continue the odyssey begun so long ago. It is mainly for

you that this book exists.

# Contents

# Illustrations

# Preface

MEMORIES ELBOWED their way forward in the 1940s as Angela Hutchinson Hammer's two index fingers flew across the ancient keyboard of her Denmore typewriter. These two fingers could type faster than most people's ten. She had a promise to keep, a promise made to her Phoenix Pen Women's group that she would record the memories of her life's journey—no small undertaking for a trip that began with the horse and buggy in 1870 and ended with the jet airplane in 1952.

Out of the old Denmore came reams of typewritten pages, a veritable treasure of early Arizona history tracing Angela's activities in mining camps, teaching in territorial schools, motherhood, homesteading, and printing and publishing small-town newspapers. Like all editors and publishers who controlled the public's only source of information, Angela helped guide Arizona's first steps into statehood; but unlike many papers financed by politicians, the railroads, or mines, Angela's papers remained independent. For twenty-eight years she managed to function in a field with little financial reward, intense competition, and exhausting workloads as she crusaded for her vision of the civic good. Despite her best efforts, she didn't quite finish her memoirs.

I am the narrator of Angela's story only because I happen to be the daughter of her eldest son Louie. Believe me, I waited as long as I could, hoping that someone else would discover my grandmother's memoirs, which had remained practically untouched in the archives at the University of Arizona and Arizona State University. Then, when the pieces of her life were practically dumped into my lap by relatives, I had no excuse but to plunge into the writing. If I delayed this project longer, I knew that time would run out for me just as it had for Angela.

I determined at the start that this book would be written for the lay reader who enjoys truthful history. As a teacher in the public secondary schools, I discovered that many students seemed to think that Arizona's pioneers were only lawmen, outlaws, ranchers, miners, or women who stayed home to darn socks and have babies. How often I had wished for lively, readable stories of the accomplishments of our early women.

For this reason, I have used dialogue and an occasional fictional device to convey information, but for the most part, Angela indicated the content of these conversations in her writing. Her own words appear in boldface type in the text. In addition, I chose not to annotate the text because my information comes mainly from Angela's memoirs on file at both state universities; old newspapers at the capitol archives; the memory banks of relatives, including my geologist brother, Don Hammer, who never forgets anything; general reading as listed in the bibliography; and my personal knowledge of my grandmother. Most of the photos and illustrations herein come from family archives. My brother Don drafted the maps.

Unfortunately, I didn't get to share in my grandmother's special brand of wisdom, since I knew her only in my youth. When she died in 1952, I was all wrapped up in college, marriage, and myself.

I grew up thinking that all grandmothers dashed around the country on Greyhound buses the way mine did. When I asked Dad why Gramma didn't drive a car, he told me that during her *Casa Grande Dispatch* days she had owned a Model-T Ford, the kind that had to be started with a crank. Always under the pressure of deadlines, she would leave the car's engine running as she sprinted up and down the street talking to people and conducting business in stores. Inevitably, some scoundrel would hop into her Model-T and drive away with it. Gramma had vowed never to drive again.

Although Gramma wasn't one for overt shows of affection, I well remember my feelings of anticipation and relief whenever I spotted her well-groomed gray head in Dad's '36 Chrysler Airstream. She would tell exciting stories, look over my artwork, and be fully present with my brother and me in a way that most adults weren't. After my mother died, Gramma represented a safety and security that was sometimes missing from my childhood.

I never doubted the love between Gramma and Dad, but after a day or two of visiting, their heated debates often continued well into the night. The next morning they would either make amends or Gramma would haughtily march to the bus station, suitcase in hand, refusing a ride in Dad's Chrysler. She would be back. They would agree to disagree about philosophical and political matters. I thought all grownups argued this way.

I first began to suspect that my grandmother was a little different on the day our country dropped the bomb on Hiroshima. Gramma's face turned ashen as she listened to the radio.

"Weren't they evil people?" I asked.

"All life is sacred, Betty. Those Japanese people are no different from you and me. Governments have to use propaganda to portray their cause as just and their enemies as evil. Otherwise, we'd never be able to drop bombs on cities and kill innocent people."

Gramma was working on her memoirs during the summer of the bomb, and she often read her stories aloud. I was ten and didn't understand much of the content, just picked up on her intonation and gestures. She talked so much about conniving men, special interests, and underhanded schemes that I later began to wonder if she wasn't a bit paranoid.

Then, after delving into Arizona history in an effort to fit the pieces of Gramma's writing together, I realized that she really had been in the line of fire. Not only was she seen as an easy target for unscrupulous men, but in the mad scramble to capitalize on Arizona's finite water, land, and mineral resources in the early part of the twentieth century, lots of shady deals took place, both within and without the halls of governance. (Did I hear you say, "What's new?") I also learned how easy it is to underestimate and take for granted those family members who are close to us.

If not for free-press guardians with courage and integrity like Gramma, where would we be today? I'm just glad she didn't live to see her beloved "fourth estate" and other media come under the control of a handful of conglomerates whereby the voices of individual journalists are often silenced or put into a straitjacket.

I hope you enjoy reading about this courageous woman and her tales of fellow settlers who developed and helped stabilize an arid environment for those of us who came later.

# Acknowledgments

MY HEARTFELT THANKS to Jack and Mildred Hammer, Mary Alice Hammer, Bill and Betty Lou Hammer, Brian McDonald, and Eleanor Bell for searching their memories and their storerooms, and to Karl Schiller for his records search in Colorado and Nevada. A special thanks to my eldest brother, Don Hammer, for the untold hours he spent reading, critiquing, drawing maps, and dispensing expert geological advice. To Dr. Henry Dobyns goes my undying gratitude for helping me navigate the muddy political waters of the Gila River. I am particularly indebted to my dear friend and fellow author Toby Heathcotte for pulling me along the writer's path, while I kicked and screamed every step of the way, and to Mona McCroskey for her encouragement and infectious love of Arizona history. I am deeply grateful to Patti Hartmann and all the reviewers of the many versions of my manuscript at the University of Arizona Press for their continuous support and for not giving up on me. I also wish to thank Sally Bennett, copy editor extraordinaire, for keying into my thought processes and making my often-convoluted sentences more readable.

Most of all, I wish to thank the Phoenix Pen Women of long ago for encouraging Angela to record her memoirs in the first place.

~ Introduction

THAT LITTLE VOICE had tried to warn Angela not to trust the banker, but as usual she hadn't listened. The idea of eliminating her competition had been too potent to resist, so she had used her printing machinery as collateral on a loan to buy out her competition, the *Bulletin*. Too late she realized it had been a scheme to put her out of business. Now she had lost everything.

The banker dropped by the *Dispatch* office to offer sympathy, but Angie knew he had come to gloat. He patted her on the head and told her that she would eventually see that her loss was for the best. "Good little women aren't cut out for newspaper work."

"No! You're very wrong! You've overlooked one thing that wasn't included in the mortgage." She pulled out the subscription list and waved it in the air. "This is the soul of the *Dispatch*, and I intend to keep it."

"You must be crazy to think you can get away with this!" With that, he stalked out of the office and stood on the sidewalk a few moments before coming back and addressing Angie in a more conciliatory tone. "How much will you take for that list?"

"Two thousand dollars cash and no less!" She hesitated. "On second thought, my subscription list isn't for sale at any price!"

"Now I know you're crazy! You're done for in this town! I'll see to it that you never set foot in the newspaper business again!"

Angie had to start over in 1914, wondering if the banker was right. Maybe she was crazy to think she could go against the wishes of town fathers and invade Arizona's small inner circle of newspapermen. Many thought this "good little woman" had stepped into an enterprise where she had no right to be, but Angela didn't place limitations on herself or allow societal norms to limit her. After each setback, she managed to find the inner strength to reinvent herself and move on.

Angela's mother, who had been a schoolteacher herself, had seen to it that Angie and her sisters had a good education in Catholic schools and convents. So, in 1905, after a dissolved marriage and desperate for a way to feed her children, Angela bought a hand press, a few fonts of type, and some ink and began printing a little tabloid called the *Wickenburg Miner*.

In her naiveté, Angela never dreamed that this purchase would place her squarely in the forefront of power struggles within the fledgling communities her newspapers would serve. Filtering each controversy though her lens of "the greatest good for the greatest number," her editorials often didn't sit well with those who had personal agendas.

In addition to juggling the newspaper business with the needs of her family, Angela homesteaded, ran for public office before most women in the nation had the right to vote, served as the immigration commissioner for Pinal County, was influential in water issues, and became a political activist.

After Angela's death in 1952, the newspaper industry paid tribute to her contributions in community building and triumphs over hardship by selecting her as the first woman to enter the Arizona Newspaper Hall of Fame. The state's Woman's Hall of Fame inducted Angela into their ranks in 1983, an honor bestowed on women whose efforts contributed substantially to the state's progress and development.

~ *Angela Hutchinson Hammer*

# ONE

## ～ Angela Comes to Arizona Territory

AFTER A THREE-DAY TRAIN JOURNEY from Reno, Nevada, the Hutchinson girls were unprepossessing when they arrived at the Casa Grande depot one July morning in 1883 to await a father they had not seen in over four long years. The quartet descended the portable stairs in birth order with a statuesque, rather dour-looking, eighteen-year-old named Mary Genevieve leading the way. After Gen came twelve-year-old Angela with serious hazel eyes, long yellow braids, and a wayward derby hat that shifted positions each time she took a step. Next in line, Mary Patricia, a year younger than Angie and dressed identically, bounced down the stairs; her derby nestled securely into thick blond curls. These hats, a great source of merriment among the girls, were part of an Easter trousseau their mother had sent to the convent along with a note saying that derbies were the latest fashion among the young set in Pinal City. Nine-year-old Mary Adelaide trailed behind Pattie, looking rather wan and unsteady on her feet, her dress bearing evidence of a nose that had bled profusely throughout the sweltering trip across the Mohave Desert.

No sooner had Addie reached ground level than an impatient porter unceremoniously heaved their luggage onto the wooden platform as if to hurry their departure from the passenger car. The locomotive gathered steam and began to inch forward as passengers crowded around train windows calling out words of assurance and waving goodbye to the girls, who stood motionless among their scattered trunks as if in a daze.

"Watch out for them giant prairie dogs, Darlin'!" one passenger yelled to Pattie.

The previous day on the train, as Pattie exclaimed over "the prairie dogs that sit up in their holes like little people," this man had jokingly informed her that "many prairie dogs weigh a ton." Urged on by other passengers, our gullible girl had spent the rest of the day at a train window searching for a giant prairie dog.

She called back, "Now I get the joke. Many prairie dogs TOGETHER weigh a ton." But her words, drowned out by the locomotive's farewell whistle, didn't reach the ears of her intended recipient.

Angie gave her sister's sweat-soaked waist an approving squeeze as together they watched their last link to civilization disappear over a mesquite-studded horizon.

At a makeshift office displaying Western Union, Wells-Fargo, and Southern Pacific Railroad signs, Angie found Gen engaged in conversation with the ticket agent. The man, seemingly confused by the appearance of four young girls on his watch, listened as Gen explained that their father was on his way from Pinal City to pick them up.

The agent allowed as how Pinal City was a good sixty miles or so from Casa Grande and told them that their papa would have had to travel all night in order to arrive this morning. He apologized for the lack of a shaded waiting area while upending the girls' trunks for temporary seating. "How was the trip from Sacramento?" he asked.

This question elicited a barrage of complaints and finger pointing at Gen, whose absentmindedness had caused them to be put off the train at Indio, California. Prior to boarding the Central Pacific train in Reno, the girls had stayed with friends of their parents, the Judge Young family. Then, after switching trains at Sacramento, Gen discovered she had left their Southern Pacific tickets behind at the Youngs'. A concerned conductor assured them that if they wired the judge for ticket confirmation, another train would be along in the morning.

Angie launched into a description of the miserable night they had spent in Indio, a place akin to Hades in her estimation. "We ate at a greasy spoon restaurant with forks and spoons made out of tin. It was so hot we couldn't sleep, and on top of that, we had indigestion all night."

Gen bore the chastisement of her sisters in silence, but when the agent went back into his office, she resumed her role as the imperial eldest. "I wish you girls would quit complaining and be thankful for the blessing of train travel.

Mary Adelaide Hutchinson (Addie), at left, around age seventeen; and Angela Hutchinson (Angie), around age twenty.

Mary Patricia Hutchinson (Pattie) in her twenties.

Mary Monica Hutchinson
(Quita) in her twenties.

How would you like to have made this trip by stage the way Mama and Baby
Monica did?"

Angie concurred with Gen, then turned her attention to their immediate
surroundings, which were not very prepossessing, either. Across a road to
the south that ran parallel to the railroad tracks stood a dreary assortment of
wooden buildings: a livery stable, a general merchandise store, a restaurant,
and one adobe hotel with a few horses and wagons tethered in front. Little
sign of life could be seen at this early hour. Well-worn wagon trails fanned out
in every direction from the railroad yard, testifying to Casa Grande's status as
a supply and shipping center for area mines and for the Indian agency at Sacaton. As far as the eye could see lay vast stretches of desert ringed by distant
mountain ranges.

To the west, a rosy, flat-topped mountain glowed in the early morning sunlight. "It's called Table Top Mountain," the agent said. "A big, Amazon woman
lives there in a cave with her tubercular husband. When we were laying these

tracks, she would sneak in at night to steal the rails, then we'd have to go out there the next day to buy them back." He chuckled. "We could have had her arrested, but we felt kind of sorry for her having to work so hard to make a few pennies."

Papa, better known as William Tallentyre Hutchinson, hurried to reach his daughters before their anxieties turned into a fear of abandonment. So often had they heard their mother, Sarah, tell the story of her own father's disappearance during California's Gold Rush that William knew well how this fear pervaded the whole family psyche.

When a distant spot of dust materialized into an approaching wagon, the girls began to clap and jump up and down. "There he is! There's our Papa!"

However, their cheers turned into stunned silence when the wagon's driver passed by with hardly a glance in their direction. He traveled down the road a short distance, then turned his team around and came slowly toward them. Stopping alongside the platform, the grinning, heavily bearded driver jumped down and rubbed his fists into his eyes as if awakening from a dream. "I had no idea that you beautiful young ladies were the same wee girls I left in Virginia City four years ago. I didn't recognize you!"

Squealing with delight, the girls mobbed their father, hugging him and chiding him for having such a short memory. He exclaimed over each daughter, making them say their names in turn to be sure these stunning beauties really belonged to him.

When the excitement abated and luggage was loaded into the wagon, William led his brood to a nearby Chinese restaurant, where they feasted on a breakfast of stale eggs, bacon, and toast with butter poured from a pickle jar, a breakfast later lost over the sides of the jouncing wagon.

Traveling in a northeasterly direction to the town of Florence, William's wagon bumped through rocky basin land, up and down arroyos, and over dry lakebeds topped with curling mud that looked like pieces of a giant puzzle. The thousands of black, fuzzy worms that crawled in every direction along the desert floor soon caught the attention of the girls. They took turns trying to flick the worms with a buggy whip to make them curl up and jump, but the fun ended when Pattie complained that they were causing pain to God's innocent creatures.

By the time the sun reached its zenith, Addie's nosebleeds began in earnest, and everyone admitted to feeling a little faint and nauseated from the heat.

After his all-night trek, William could hardly keep his eyes open. He pulled in to the Florence Hotel for a long afternoon siesta during the hottest part of the day.

The proprietor of the hotel, kind Dixie Whitlaw Stone, led the girls to an adobe addition that looked as if it might have been formerly used as a fortress. Over large openings on three sides, Dixie hung dripping wet blankets. The effect of desert breezes blowing across these wet blankets, a time-honored system of evaporative cooling, soon lulled the tired, hot girls into restful slumber.

Lengthening afternoon shadows found the Hutchinson family under way for the long haul to Pinal City. Upon leaving the flat desert basin, the wagon team labored up mountainous grades into higher and greener elevations. Cactus spines, backlit by the setting sun, shimmered under waxy crowns of red, yellow, pink, and mauve in the last stages of bloom. Angie exclaimed, "This is not at all the way I had pictured the desert. The nuns taught us that deserts were barren and sandy, but this one is full of vegetation. I love it already."

As night fell, young imaginations stirred to strange sights and sounds. Clumps of saguaros become road agents pointing guns at the wagon, or the towering smokestacks of mill towns, or companies of soldiers marching with muskets over their shoulders. Bunches of fluffy chollas turned into flocks of sheep resting on a hillside.

Imaginations lapsed into drowsiness as the vast silence of a moonless night settled across the land, a silence occasionally interrupted by the howling of coyotes, the hooting of owls, or the sleepy voices of adolescents asking the age-old question, "How far is it now, Papa?"

At about a mile east of the point where the Boyce Thompson Arboretum is today, Gen spotted a row of dark buildings on her side of the road. "Papa, you didn't tell us that Pinal City had skyscrapers."

William chuckled. "Those buildings are the bank and the newspaper office. They look tall because they're built on the slope of a hill." He called attention to a huge, dark building on the opposite side of the road. "That's the mill where I work, where the ore from the Silver King Mine is treated. It has eight stamps, and when it's in operation, it makes a deafening roar."

Wide-awake, the girls strained for a first glimpse of their new home. The wagon took a diagonal course to the right and stopped in front of a building that even in the darkness appeared very drab. No one moved until they saw the glow of a candle coming toward them and heard their mother's voice.

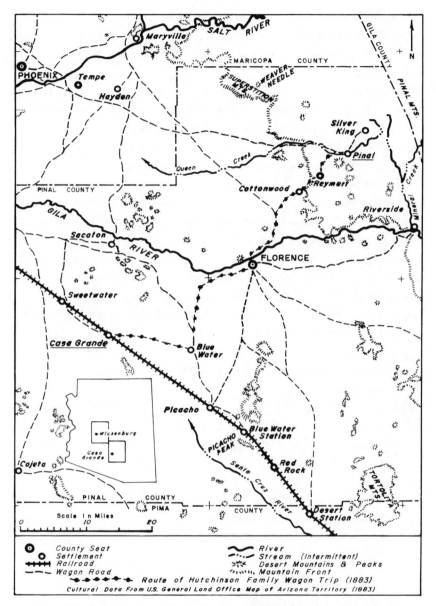

Portions of Pinal and Maricopa Counties showing the route of the Hutchinson family from Casa Grande to Pinal City, 1883. (Map by Donald F. Hammer, modified from an 1883 U.S. General Land Office map of the Territory of Arizona)

The anxiety caused by long separation melted into tears of joy as Sarah inspected each daughter by candlelight and saw that even her younger daughters carried the unmistakable signs of approaching puberty. She was shocked at this change.

Right away the girls wanted to see their baby sister, but little Monica (called Quita) slept through all the hubbub of the happy reunion. Sarah warned the girls not to be disappointed if Monica didn't remember them.

Though the hour was well past midnight, the family sat down to their first meal together in over four years. Each girl returned her fervent thanks to the Lord for this long-awaited reunion, and then nonstop talking erupted from all sides of the table. At the end of the meal, Sarah came from the kitchen carrying a can of Borden's Sweetened Condensed Milk, a new product on the market, with four spoons. Everyone agreed it tasted like nectar of the gods.

As heads began to nod, Sarah led the girls to their new sleeping quarters, where four cots stood side by side. William, who made most of the family's furnishings, had fashioned these cots from canvas stretched over crossed two-by-four legs, and once Angie discovered how easily these cots could be folded up, she proclaimed her father a genius.

While the girls got ready for bed, Sarah warned them to be alert for scorpions. Bedcovers should be shaken and the walls and ceiling checked before climbing into bed.

Angie picked up her cot. "Look! I can just fold up my bed and walk to a different spot if I see a scorpion on the ceiling."

Despite her bravado, Angie slept fitfully that night. Each time her skin brushed a raw edge of canvas, she startled awake, thinking it was the legs of a scorpion.

At the first rays of light, Angie scrambled out of bed to see her baby sister, only to be disappointed by an unenthusiastic reception. Little Monica didn't remember her and shyly trailed at arm's length as Angie took inventory of her new home.


## At Home in Pinal City

William Hutchinson, a steam engineer by trade, built and operated the huge stamp mills used in the mining industry for crushing gold and silver ore. As part of the great horde of mining men who migrated from one mineral discovery to the next along the Comstock and other parts of Nevada, he and Sarah lived a nomadic lifestyle. Like clockwork at each mining camp, a baby had arrived: Gen and Joseph at Virginia City, Angela at Hamilton, Pattie at Piermont, Addie at Egan Canyon, and five years later, Mary Monica at Monterey, California. When the mines of the Comstock began to decline, and after the tragic drowning death of Joseph (his only son), William came to the Arizona Territory in 1879 to look for new mining opportunities.

Settling in Picket Post, later renamed Pinal City, he opened a blacksmith shop while awaiting employment at the Silver King concentrator. Sarah and Baby Monica joined him there in 1881, after leaving the other four girls in a convent in Virginia City until the Apache troubles abated.

With Sarah's arrival, William added another bedroom and a kitchen to the same building that had housed his former blacksmith shop. Unable to afford glass, he covered the window and door openings of the new additions with unbleached muslin tacked onto frames. The older part of the building served as the parlor, where a pine-board table surrounded by upholstered beer barrels sat upon a floor of rough-hewn planks. A bookcase contained the family's most important possession, their library. Tightly drawn, wine-colored draperies, a remnant of more affluent days in Virginia City, covered the parlor's single glass window.

The town of Pinal City grew around the Silver King quartz mill, constructed in 1878, along a bank of Queen Creek. Commercial buildings such as a shoe shop, M. Jacobs and Company, Goldman's General Merchandise, Murray's Saloon, and the Carroll Sisters' Hotel and Restaurant faced a plaza containing the town well. Since William had built his blacksmith shop in the business district, it, too, fronted the plaza.

According to Sarah, all kinds of wickedness took place in the plaza. People used language not fitting for the ears of young girls. Drunks came out of saloons to fistfight or sleep off binges. Lowborn women gathered to gossip instead of seeing to their children, and occasionally, gangs of cowboys, a vernacular for "toughs," rode around on horseback looking for someone to pick on. If the toughs found a newcomer and didn't like his looks or the kind of hat he wore, they would shoot at his feet to make him dance.

"Furthermore," Sarah told her daughters, "our parlor drapes are to remain closed at all times. You are not even to look upon the plaza through the front window. Now come around to the back of the house where Papa has built a nice seesaw and swing for you." There, Sarah had one more ground rule to establish. She called anything beyond a sandy wash skirting this playground the "badlands," and the girls were forbidden to cross it.

One morning, to Angie's and Pattie's surprise, Sarah handed them each a five-gallon oilcan fitted with wooden crossbars for handles and told them to fetch water from the plaza well. "You'll find a bucket with a rope attached at the well. Just lower this bucket into the water and pull it up hand over hand. You'll catch on. When your cans are full, come right back home. Don't dawdle."

At the well, three women deeply engaged in gossip watched the girls' clumsy attempts to pull up the water-filled bucket. One of the women came to their aid. As she demonstrated how to pull the bucket up in a steady motion, she continued talking about Black Jack, a local saloon entertainer who lived a life of shame in order to support her two young daughters in a Tucson convent.

Angie and Pattie discussed Black Jack's situation all the way home. They concluded that someone needed to tell the woman to run away and stay at the convent with her daughters. Angie said, "Black Jack probably doesn't know that the nuns would be glad to help her. Let's try to find her and tell her ourselves, since we've had firsthand experience with nuns and convents."

From that day on, Angie and Pattie took up surveillance on the plaza, hoping to somehow spot a woman who might be Black Jack. They hid between the forbidden window and the wine-colored draperies while other members of the household took their afternoon siestas.

Another task given to the girls was that of bringing milk from a dairy across Queen Creek where a large cottonwood tree that had fallen across the creek offered a challenging shortcut. The girls hauled their milk can around branches while the creek, swollen from monsoon rains, raged beneath them. In the big muddy root, they dug footholds and handholds so they could climb over it and slide to the bank on the far side. For the return trip, they used a rope to pull the milk can over the root end, then passed the can from girl to girl in bucket-brigade fashion.

One day a mill hand happened to be standing at the doorway of the Silver King concentrator and saw the girls making their way along the tree bridge with the milk can. He called William. "Come and take a look at what your youngsters are doing."

The girls received stern lectures from both parents that evening. Their bodies could be torn apart by floodwaters if they happened to fall, or even worse, their bodies might never be found. One drowning in the family was enough.

The next day the girls discovered a two-by-four handrail nailed along the length of their tree bridge. Their shortcut to Rudledge's Diary lost its attraction once the element of danger had been removed.


## A Synthetic Cowboy

Gen had been engaged twice and jilted twice before she left Nevada. As the eligible new girl in town, she was under scrutiny by every lonely bachelor in the vicinity of Pinal City. She made her town debut when the local Catholic community held a bazaar for the church building fund. Gen was in charge of the lemonade stand.

One very handsome young man kept returning to Gen's stand to buy drinks for himself and his buddies. He introduced himself as Ned Fales and removed his hat in a great show of respect. Although Gen had heard that Fales had a fiancée, she allowed him to help her squeeze lemons. By the end of the day, Gen's stand had outstripped all others as the bazaar's big moneymaker.

That evening Gen told her mother she considered Ned Fales to be quite a gentleman. Sarah harrumphed and launched into her opinion of the young man. "He's nothing but a synthetic cowboy from a wealthy Missouri family who indulge his fantasy of becoming an Indian fighter. He brags around town that he'll send old Geronimo's scalp home to his parents."

Upon hearing this, Angie and Pattie added Ned Fales to their surveillance list. So far, they hadn't seen anyone who fit the description of Black Jack, only old weathered prospectors who brought gunnysacks of black sand to the well and used steer horns, instead of gold pans, to separate any gold flakes from the sand. Then, just when they began to think their mother had greatly exaggerated the dangers of the plaza, they witnessed an event that sent them scurrying back to their cots, feigning sleep.

Amid the sound of loud, angry voices, Ned Fales himself strode out the swinging doors of Murray's Saloon. Even at a distance Angie and Pattie could tell he was angry. Another man, who stood in the doorway shouting obscenities, fired a pistol at Fales' retreating back. The young tough staggered momentarily, then drew his pistol, whirled around, and fired. The man in the doorway collapsed onto the boardwalk.

Mary Genevieve
Hutchinson (Gen) taught in
the Vulture City School in
1886.

When Murray's clients streamed out of the saloon yelling for an officer of
the law, Fales made no attempt to run. He sheathed his pistol and sat on the
edge of the well with his head in his hands to await the lawman. Angie and
Pattie didn't wait to see what happened next.

William reported two different versions of the killing of Bill O'Boyle, a
highly respected owner of a hotel and restaurant in Silver King. In one version,
Ned Fales started the fight by accusing O'Boyle of circulating rumors that he
had participated in a train robbery, whereupon O'Boyle threw a glass of beer
in Fales' face. Fales started to leave the tavern, then changed his mind and shot
O'Boyle at close range. The other version had Fales punching O'Boyle in re-
taliation for the rumors, then leaving the saloon. Some of Murray's patrons
claimed that O'Boyle, who had been drinking all afternoon, fired a shot over
Fales' head to scare him as he walked away.

Either way, William figured Fales had already been convicted of murder
in cold blood and doubted that the cowboy, who had a bad reputation for
drunken forays into town, could get a fair trial in Pinal City. The loudest voice

to proclaim Fales' guilt came from Jack McCoy, O'Boyle's brother-in-law, a man rumored to be in love with Ned Fales' fiancée.

Gen retired early with a headache, leaving Angie and Pattie to wash dishes. Alone in the kitchen, they briefly discussed telling their parents what they had seen that afternoon but decided against the severe spanking that would surely follow such an admission. Besides, other adults had witnessed the incident and would certainly tell the truth.

That night a lynch mob, led by Jack McCoy, got the keys away from the jailer, took Fales to a nearby barn, and hung him from the rafters. When his body was cut down the next morning, the coroner discovered that a gunshot wound had grazed the flesh in his side, indisputable proof that Ned Fales had acted in self-defense.

As Angela looked back on the young cowboy's funeral sixty-three years later, she vividly recalled the moonlit night and the coffin in the open grave under the spreading branches of a mesquite tree. She wrote about the funeral, held a few miles up Silver King Road at Jimmy Reymert's place.

**The entire population of Pinal City came to protest the illegal death of a man on hearsay evidence. As the first clods of dirt hit the wooden casket, the minister asked the Almighty to touch the hearts of the sinners and forgive the penitents. A large clump of beautiful and poisonous jimson weed exuded its sickly fragrance into the night air, a fitting touch to the occasion.**

**Ned Fales became the tragic figure who might have become a good, substantial citizen had he not indulged in horseplay and been hated by his rivals. Jack McCoy suffered remorse for his part in the hanging, motivated more by jealousy than revenge. He often talked to Mother about his regrets.**

## Glass Snakes and Arizona Diamonds

Each evening, Gen held court in the parlor. Her suitors came bearing gifts — nuggets of white quartz with thin silver wires curled together like bird's nests, possibly high-grade from the Silver King Mine, and all sorts of filigreed silver jewelry made by local Mexican craftsmen. Occasionally, Sarah allowed Gen to go walking with an admirer, provided one or more of her sisters trailed along, a task they found most disagreeable.

Sarah approved of Pat Donahue, a seemingly good Irish Catholic boy, so Gen accepted his invitation to the St. Patrick's Day Ball. Pat pressed his luck by announcing to Sarah that he didn't want any sisters tagging along to the dance. The parlor turned silent. No one had ever dared talk to the diminutive Sarah this way.

When Sarah found her voice, she issued a surprising command: "You must prove to me that you are worthy of my daughter's company and a man of true faith by getting down on your knees and reciting three Decades of the Rosary for me."

The parlor audience gasped, not believing for a second that Pat would put his pride on the line by acquiescing to this command. But to their surprise, he slowly knelt before Sarah and took the rosary from her hands. Then, after inviting the whole household on their knees along with him, he reeled off the Rosaries like an altar boy.

Sarah had no choice but to relent, and the erstwhile tagalongs breathed a sigh of relief. However, she extracted one last promise from the couple. They must agree not to participate in any round dances. It was considered improper for dancers to have bodily contact.

As the eldest of the siblings, Gen had always functioned as a surrogate mother. Now, with her attention diverted by suitors, the younger girls took advantage of their freedom by exploring farther and farther up Queen Creek with their Hispanic playmates.

August of 1883 brought terrific storms to the area. *The Pinal Drill* reported that J. D. Reymert's rain box measured over thirteen inches of rain in one two-hour period. Homes and livestock close to the creek bed were swept away by its raging waters.

Angie wrote poignantly of Queen Creek, their favorite playground.

**It was a wide and, at times, turbulent stream that ripped out everything in its path when the summer rains swept over the mountains in sheets that seemed to be almost horizontal.**

**Mother always said they came in honor of the Feast of the Assumption. As mother was a devout Catholic, we usually observed those particular days in church; but there was no church in Pinal, so someone donated the use of their home for services.**

**The creek cut through some of the roughest country imaginable, where it**

Pinal City, circa 1880. View northwestward showing Queen Creek in flood.
The Silver King concentrator is at the left edge of the photograph.
(Courtesy of the Sharlot Hall Museum)

**was compelled to make more than an ordinary display of foam to get through narrow gorges. It washed clean any rock ledges impeding its way, but left something behind of interest to us children in the way of odd-looking rocks.**

The youngsters, having heard so many of Sarah's Irish legends, made up stories about the rocks that had what looked like glass snakes inside. These snakes were the ones that St. Patrick drove out of Ireland by locking them into crystal-lined rocks and throwing them into the ocean. After rolling around on the ocean floor for hundreds of years, the rocks tumbled their way to Queen Creek. Their father called these snake rocks *geodes*.

Farther up the creek, the girls found a hill of "Arizona diamonds": translucent, coffee-colored nodules of obsidian that looked like beads. These Arizona diamonds made their way back to the house in such numbers that they were swept under furniture or out the door.

On another exploratory trip, the girls found an abandoned quartz mill that had been used to concentrate ore for Judge Reymert's Seventy-six Mine. They collected handfuls of quicksilver, or mercury, from the mill's amalgamation plates used to process precious metals from ore. When William caught them playing with the quicksilver, he told them to return it to the mill. Quicksilver was expensive, and Judge Reymert might want to use it again someday; besides, they had no business taking things that didn't belong to them. No one considered that quicksilver might be toxic.

Not far from the old mill, Judge Reymert was building a great stone castle on a hillside. Each afternoon, the girls went to watch the judge's daughter-in-law feed the castle cats with chunks of salt pork cut from a big slab. Never completed, the castle stood ghostlike for years and became known as "Reymert's Folly."

Fearless Pattie, always ready for a snake attack, carried a rope with her on the day the girls and their playmates tried to hike to the Superstition Mountains, a distance of some fifteen to twenty miles. When they got to the wide gorge skirting the mountain, Pattie spied the head of a Gila monster protruding from some rocks. She dropped a slipknot loop over its head, slung it over her shoulder, and ordered everyone back home. Despite pleas from the Hispanic children to let the reptile go, Pattie persevered with her burden. By the time they reached home, the Gila monster was nearly dead, and the girls came away from the adventure with another lecture from William about the dangers of reptiles and their perceptions of distance.

On San Juan's Day, June 24th, the Hutchinson family joined others in Pinal City for mariachi music, dancing, food, and games on the plaza. One of the festival highlights was a game called *saca el gallo*, in which live chickens were buried in the ground up to their necks. Two teams of horsemen competed to see which team could pull the most chickens out of the ground. Only the most expert horseman could grab the ducking head of a chicken by hanging way off the side of his saddle. The rider that accomplished this feat then used the chicken like a baseball bat to whack his opponents about the head and shoulders. Blood and feathers flew everywhere. The horrified expressions on the faces of the Hutchinson girls only added to the amusement of the riders.

Thus the Hutchinson girls grew accustomed to life in Pinal City. Color lines blurred, and soon Angie couldn't tell the difference between her own sunburned skin and that of her Hispanic playmates.

William's gentle, retiring nature stood in sharp contrast to his tiny wife's prideful ways and often-fiery disposition. The couple came from opposite ends of the religious and political spectrum: he, from a Southern family of slave owners and Protestant English patriots, and she, from an Irish Catholic family of globe-trotting adventurers and explorers. William generally acquiesced to Sarah's wishes, except for the time he went prospecting over her objections.

Pinal buzzed with the news of mineral discoveries in the Quijotoa Mountains west of Tucson. If Sarah could spare him for a few weeks, it wouldn't take William long to stake a few claims in the region.

She wouldn't hear of it. "You can't go by yourself. Besides, I hear those Pimas and Papagos are getting a little hostile about all the ranchers and prospectors invading their land. You can't be taking off on your own when you have family responsibilities."

That put an end to this discussion for the time being. Then Willie, the son of Judge Young in Reno, came for a visit with gold on his mind. He begged William to take him prospecting. William resisted until Jose, a young Papago (those Indians now called the Tohono O'odham), told him that he knew where there was "heaps of gold" in the Quijotoa Mountains. That did it. Over Sarah's objections, the three men put together a pack outfit and took off.

It's uncertain how long they were gone, but by the time William limped home empty handed to an angry wife, he found that he had also lost his job at the Silver King Mill.

The search for a new job began as the recalcitrant William trekked from one mine to the next. At each mine, he heard the same story. Due to a drop in silver prices, companies were laying off workers. Eventually, he found employment at the Monarch of the Sea, a prospect about a half-mile above the Silver King Mine.

The family took temporary quarters at the William's Hotel, located in the Silver King settlement near the waste dump. While there, a guest happened to catch a six-inch centipede in a glass jar. In those days, people feared centipedes as much as scorpions, believing that if a centipede's legs pierced the skin, it would cause the flesh to rot away. Onlookers began telling centipede stories, and William joined in with one about the time a nine-inch centipede dropped from the ceiling on top of Sarah as she lay in bed. It took all the courage Sarah could muster not to scream or move as the critter slowly traversed her entire body before finally dropping to the floor. From that day forward, Angie considered her mother to be the bravest woman on the planet.

William didn't remain at Monarch of the Sea long. The prospect closed in a few months, and William left Silver King in late 1884 or early 1885 to look for work in Maricopa County.

Mormon colonization of Arizona had become one of the most hotly debated topics of the time. But public sentiment against the Church of Latter-Day Saints didn't prevent Sarah from purchasing farm produce from Mr. Vance, who made frequent rounds to Pinal City from his farm in Mesa. When the time came for the family to move to Phoenix, Sarah asked Mr. Vance if he would transport Gen, Angie, Pattie, and Addie to Phoenix to look for housing while she stayed behind to pack.

The trip to Mesa took two days. The first night, spent on the ground at Hewitt's Station, found Gen anxious about snakes and hydrophobic skunks. Mr. Vance and his dog stayed awake to keep watch.

The next night, the girls stayed at the Vance home before continuing on to Phoenix. Still in the process of developing farmland, Mr. Vance had built a comfortable home along an ancient canal originally constructed by the Hohokam Indians to channel water from the Salt River. The family's drinking water came from this irrigation ditch, and even though the water was strained and put into ollas to cool, Angie noted that it still had a muddy taste.

After supper that evening, Gen and Mr. Vance launched into a discussion of the Bible and the teachings of Brigham Young and Joseph Smith. To clear the air of any negativity, Gen told how a kind Mormon neighbor had saved her mother's life in Egan Canyon, Nevada. After giving birth to Addie, Sarah had been on the verge of death from excessive hemorrhaging when this Mormon woman packed her with snow to staunch the bleeding. "Ever since then," Gen told the Vances, "Mother will not permit an unkind word to be spoken about Mormons in her presence."

In Phoenix, the girls found a vacant adobe house near the Linville Addition, not far from the old courthouse. Angie said that this abandoned home's well-worn floors and woodwork and its surrounding giant cottonwood trees gave one the feeling of barging in on a prehistoric civilization. When Sarah arrived, she didn't want to remain in this house without the consent of the owners, so the family underwent a series of moves that ended in a house rented from Mr. Fifield, across the street from the Old Town Ditch with its row of mud-roofed adobes.

Apparently, William didn't find work in Phoenix, and by the time his family arrived there, he had found employment at the Vulture Mine about sixty miles northwest of Phoenix. Knowing that Gen had a teaching certificate from Mount St. Mary's, the Catholic convent in Reno where the girls had stayed, he wrote Gen that the Vulture City School might soon need a teacher. She should come to investigate and bring Angie along with her. Protocol of the day deemed it improper for young ladies to travel alone.

## A Room at Hannah's

By the time William found employment as a stamp mill steam engineer at the Vulture Mine in 1885, this mine, touted as the richest in Arizona, already had a long and notorious history. It was the classic story of Henry Wickenburg, a poor prospector, finding a rich quartz vein in the late 1860s and losing it to eastern capitalists. However, Wickenburg's discovery of gold brought miners and settlers to a remote region of central Arizona that had been occupied solely by Indians.

After Henry and his companions formed a mining district, he allowed any comers to pack off the rich gold ore at fifteen dollars a ton. Miners carried this ore to the Hassayampa River, ten miles due east of the Vulture. Soon *arrastras*, great stone wheels used to crush ore, lined the riverbank. This camp became known as Wickenburg and would eventually become the town of Wickenburg.

In 1866 the Vulture Mining Company contracted to pay Henry twenty-five thousand dollars for his ownership interest and built a twenty-stamp mill and company houses at a place on the river they called Vulture City. (This was not the same Vulture City that later grew around the Vulture Mine.)

Stockholders in the Vulture Mining Company received little return on their investment. Freighters charged eight to ten dollars a ton to haul ore, so only choice rock was sent to the mill, a practice that made it easy for miners and freighters to pocket high-grade along the way.

Boilers for steam engines at the mill burned lots of wood. When the company ran out of a wood supply at Vulture City I, the company erected another ten-stamp mill, Smith's Mill, twelve miles south of the original Vulture City. At this mill, they installed a flume to carry water from the Hassayampa River. The cost of milling Vulture ore kept getting steeper and steeper until the Vulture Mining Company caved in.

When the Central Arizona Company took ownership of the Vulture in 1879, it moved the old mill at Vulture City to Seymour until it could complete a pipeline to carry water from the Hassayampa River all the way to the mine site. A new influx of money from investors allowed an eighty-stamp mill to be erected at the mouth of the inclined shaft that accessed the Vulture lode. A settlement, Vulture City II, grew around the company buildings at the Vulture Mine site.

By the time William arrived in this second Vulture City, the Central Arizona Company had met the same fate as the old Vulture Company, their expenses far exceeding any profits from gold. Unhappy stockholders agreed to lease the mine property to Lyman Elmore, a New York attorney. Instead of working underground, Elmore kept the mill busy processing the low-grade ore that had been stockpiled around the mine. Under these circumstances, William realized his job probably wouldn't last long.

Gen and Angie made arrangements to stay at Hannah Humphrey's Boarding House, but Angie wasn't happy to learn that Hannah's was the big social center for Vulture City. Although she had learned to polka and hop waltz at the convent, she wasn't ready to put herself on stage with a mixed crowd. Shy and awkward at sixteen, she still wore her hair in braids and considered herself a "homely brat."

This low opinion of herself came partly as the result of an incident in Virginia City when Sarah's sister had come to offer condolences after the drowning death of Angie's brother Joe. Angie described what happened.

> **I admired Aunt Norah, a large, important-looking woman who dressed like a millionaire. When she arrived, she turned to Pattie and said, "So this is the little darling who looks like me?"**
>
> **"Oh, no," piped up Gen. "Not Pattie. It's Angie who looks like you."**
>
> **Aunt Norah's face fell. I knew immediately that she was hurt and offended to think that such a plain brat could look like her.**

Angie confided her social fears to Gen, saying that she would remain in their room when people gathered in the evening to dance and converse. "With these pigtails of mine, I look like I'm twelve, instead of sixteen."

Gen laughed at her sister. "We can remedy that. You won't recognize yourself when I get through with you."

That evening a comely young lady took her place among the guests who congregated in front of Hannah's dining room fireplace. Angie's hair, arranged in a pug, sported stylish Saratoga waves around her face. She made friends with the younger set and actually took a turn or two on the dance floor. Over the next few weeks she met many residents of Vulture City: the Kirklands, the Jacksons, the Joneses, the Rances, the Osborns, and the Amaviscas.

When Gen and Angie visited Laura Copeland, the current teacher at the town's two-room schoolhouse, Laura revealed the reason for her haste in finding a replacement. She and Fred Brill, a trustee on the Vulture City School Board, were secretly engaged. They couldn't marry as long as Laura remained in the school's employ. Gen took over her teaching duties immediately.

Vulture City didn't offer much in the way of family housing, but William found a small frame house for sale on a flat below the mill. He didn't have enough cash to buy it and because of his uncertainty of continuing employment was hesitant to sign a note. There were rumors of the mine being sold to a silver baron from Colorado, who would, most likely, bring in his own personnel.

Gen talked him into signing for the loan. She reasoned that it would be less costly if the whole family lived together. "If something should happen to your job, I can make the payments on the note."

So the family came together once again to live in the little house on the flat.

With the mill's mighty stamps pounding day and night, the whole house reverberated, and conversation in a normal tone of voice was impossible. They soon got used to this constant din, and as Angie noted, when the stamps weren't in operation, the silence seemed so strange that no one could sleep.

Angie, Pattie, and Addie attended Gen's school, where most of the students were Hispanic. Gen spoke fluent Spanish, as did both parents, but the girls had picked up a lot of slang along with smatterings of the language. They often found themselves as a center of amusement when they tried to converse with their classmates.

The Kirklands owned a large general merchandise store in town, but since this store didn't stock women's apparel, Mr. Levy, the owner of a stage line, began bringing in ready-made clothing and hosiery. With no outlet for selling his goods, he talked Pattie and Addie into becoming his peddling merchants. The girls did a brisk business until competition arrived. John Hyder, another stage line owner, began bringing in huge cases of expensive women's clothing, so Mr. Levy looked about for another product to sell and hit upon the idea of importing ice cream in large, well-packed freezers.

The girls, ecstatic about turning their home into an ice cream parlor, began serving this delectable treat to the town's three hundred grateful residents. Although this venture became an instant success, the days of their ice cream parlor were numbered.

Not far from the little house on the flat, a menacing glacier of yellow mill tailings crept closer and closer each day. Neighbors abandoned their homes. Then, when the peril could no longer be ignored, the family moved to higher and safer ground, and the great wedge of yellow sand swallowed Pattie and Addie's ice cream parlor, along with all the rest of the homes below the mill.

Life didn't get dull in Vulture City. No sooner did the family settle into another frame house than trouble arrived at the mill when a former adversary of William's came to work in the boiler room on a different shift. The two men had worked together at some mill in the past and for some unknown reason had become sworn enemies. After eyeing each other warily for a few days, William extended a hand of friendship. They talked over their past problems, and both agreed "to bury the hatchet."

This truce lasted until it became apparent that the man was deliberately letting the steam boilers go dry before William's shift began. William confronted the man, who immediately flew into a rage. Greatly outweighed by his opponent, William took a bruising beating. In desperation and fearing for his life, William grabbed a pocketknife that he kept above his workbench for cutting plug tobacco. Gauging the knife blade to just the right length, he plunged it into the man's belly. After a few jabs, the man felt his blood running and backed away. William was brought home with an injured back and a face so battered that he was practically unrecognizable.

The company doctor ordered that hot packs be kept on William's back around the clock, a task that all the Hutchinson women took turns performing. Meanwhile, the assailant brought attempted murder charges against William, charges that were thrown out of court on grounds of self-defense. William couldn't return to work for six weeks.

What disturbed Angie the most about all this was that her papa enjoyed a reputation as a congenial, valued employee with excellent blacksmithing skills. Perhaps, she thought, the man who had pounded Papa was jealous of his good reputation. She noted with pride a carefully folded letter of recommendation from General Rosecrans that William carried in his wallet until the day he died. Rosecrans, who had been a major general in the Civil War, a congressman, and a minister to Mexico, had employed William at his San Jose Mine in California in the early 1860s.

Dear Sir:

I remember you very well as a mining and steam engineer at our San Jose Mill, where your services were efficient and intelligent. Anybody who knows what it is to run a twenty-stamp mill with pans and settlers such as that one and keep it going, knows that much work puts an engineer on his trial.

Your engineering was a success and to your trustworthiness and good temper, I can testify with great pleasure.

Yours truly,
W. S. Rosecrans

As a testament to William's worth, he remained among the few kept on at the mill in 1887 when Horace A. W. Tabor, the silver baron from Colorado, bought the Vulture Mine. Tabor sent a tough new engineer, Cyrus Gribble, to oversee its operation, and Gribble quickly cleaned house of all slackers. Not only did Gribble appreciate William's work ethic, the two men eventually became good friends. At last the mine seemed to be heading in the right direction.

### The Aborted Stage Holdup

After Laura Copeland married Fred Brill, Gen often spent weekends visiting at their ranch about three miles down the Hassayampa River from Wickenburg. An unexpected brush with tragedy occurred during one of these visits when two of the ranch cowboys, Leopold Walleth and Will Gore, noticed flames lighting up the southern sky. Upon investigation, the cowboys found the smoldering wagon and possessions of a neighbor, Barney Martin. Then, to their horror, the cowboys discovered the cremated remains of Barney and his whole family.

After notifying authorities, the cowboys returned to the site of the tragedy and gathered the remains of the Martin family for burial. What little they could find fit into a candle box. At the ranch, the Brills, the cowboys, Gen, and Pattie held a brief funeral service for the deceased and buried the box near a road leading from the ranch to the river.

Few people were deceived by the murderer's attempt to make the crime look like the work of Yavapai Indians by scalping or burning their victims. Angie noted,

> It was fairly well established that "Bloody" Stanton was the fiendish murderer of the Martin family. The Martins had just sold their ranch and were carrying the money, about five thousand dollars, with the intention of buying a place in the Valley.

Stanton, who ran a stage stop at the foot of Antelope Mountain near Wickenburg, kept evading the law until a group of men from Wickenburg took it upon themselves to go after him. They put him below ground in 1886.

Because of attacks by outlaws and Indians, Wells-Fargo had quit carrying the Vulture gold in the early 1880s. Therefore, each succeeding mine superintendent had to devise his own strategies for getting the bullion to Phoenix. Bandits watched every stage or rider who left Vulture, and although stage drivers normally didn't transport gold along with passengers, every conveyance came under suspicion. Apparently, this is what happened the morning that Sarah loaded Angie, Pattie, and Addie into Dick Huzy's new spring wagon for a trip to Phoenix.

When the wagon passed into a mesquite thicket not far from the Agua Fria Station, a shot ripped through the air. Dick Huzy whipped up his team, while Sarah pushed the girls to the floorboard and covered them with a comforter. Angie told what happened next.

> **The horses ran so fast that I thought the stage would either overturn or go to pieces. As we pulled into the Agua Fria Station, and it appeared no one was following us, Mother turned to Dick saying, "Tell me the truth! Are you carrying the bullion on this stage?"**
>
> **Dick seemed shocked at the question. "God, no! I would never carry bullion with passengers."**

Sarah wasn't convinced.

After giving a report at the station, Dick and Sarah were advised to spend the night and leave at an undetermined time in the morning in case another holdup was in the works.

On the return trip to Vulture, Sarah and the girls again stopped at the Agua Fria Station. Mrs. Elder, the proprietress, told Sarah that she had overheard two men discussing the holdup. She went on to say, "I didn't let on that I could understand Spanish. I recognized one of the men, Inocente Martinez. The other man asked Inocente why he only fired one shot at the stage and didn't stop it. Inocente answered, 'Por Dios, no! It had the teacher's mother and sisters on it. We'll try another time.' "

Mr. Gribble, the new mine superintendent, often visited at the Hutchinson home to talk about their common links to England and Ireland. He talked about his wife and nine children, who still lived in the Old Country. Angie recorded her memory of one of these discussions, humorously spiced with all the affectations of proper discourse.

> **"It's this way," he began, "I hardly ever get 'ome more than once a year. The devil of it is that a new baby lands after every visit. I'd like to settle down and get acquainted with my children, but the life of a mining engineer doesn't work that way."**
>
> **"Why don't you bring your family with you?" Mother asked. "I've been**

John Kennard Murphy
(J.K.), a Maricopa County
sheriff, married Genevieve
in 1888.

traipsing all over the country with William, following wherever he goes. Each of our children were born in a different mining camp in Nevada."

Mr. Gribble looked pensive as he sipped his tea. "Why don't I? Mrs. Gribble agrees that we must consider the children's education, health, and social standing. They could lose all that if we hawked them from pillar to post around the world."

"I suppose you're right, Mr. Gribble, but let me beseech you right now to be more careful of your own life in this unsettled country. I beg of you not to ever carry that bullion to Phoenix again. You have a family to think of."

"Tush, tush, don't worry about me, dear lady. I can pick off any robber before he takes aim. No highwayman's gun will ever get me. No, I'm not afraid in the least."

On March 19, 1888, Cyrus Gribble left Vulture in broad daylight with a driver and two husky guards on horseback. He carried three thousand dollars' worth of bullion in his light wagon. Angela described him as a large man who bulked high in the buggy seat with a rifle resting across his lap. He waved to the girls as he passed their house, the last time they would see him alive.

Cyrus Gribble rode into an ambush near the Agua Fria River and didn't get off a shot. The entire party fell under a fusillade of bullets.

Various posses trailed the bandits and recovered the Vulture gold. One version of the fate of Inocente Martinez appeared on the back of a picture of a handsome, young deputy sheriff who led one of the posses. Next to the sheriff's name, John Kennard Murphy, an unknown hand inscribed the following: "Married Mary Genevieve Hutchinson, 1888. Deputy sheriff of Maricopa County who trailed the Gribble murderers to an island on the Colorado River, ten miles from the Mexican border. Inocente Martinez jailed in the Territorial Prison."

# *TWO*

## ∽ Clouds Are Made of Smoke

ANGIE AND PATTIE stood discreetly aside while Ed Gill, the editor of the *Phoenix Republican*, talked to the gentleman with the flowing, red whiskers. After having heard that Gill sometimes hired female compositors, the girls had come to the office of this fledgling newspaper in the late 1880s, hoping to add a few coins to the family coffer. William had lost his job at the Vulture Mill after it fell into the hands of a British company, and the family had returned to Phoenix, settling into a rental on Tenth Street and Washington.

Editor Gill came out of the back room carrying a stack of fresh newsprint and set it on the counter. "Mr. Hadsell, I know I promised to have your flyers folded, but I'm short-handed and my printers are threatening to strike. I'm afraid you'll have to find someone else to do your folding."

Before Mr. Hadsell had time to respond, Pattie tapped him politely on the shoulder. "Excuse me, sir. We came here looking for work, and we'd be happy to fold your brochures for you."

The red whiskers broke into a smile. "Ed, why don't you put these young ladies to work if you're shorthanded? I'm most anxious to announce my new land development in Peoria, so be sure they get my work done first."

Never had Gill seen more nimble hands than those of Angie and Pattie. They kept the printers busy bringing stacks of newsprint from the basement for folding. One of the printers growled, "You aren't expected to make machines of yourselves. Do an honest day's work, but don't go overboard."

Before long the girls found themselves in the *Republican*'s composing room to learn the rudiments of setting type. At the time, it wasn't too unusual for tight-fisted editors to hire female compositors and pay them less than the wage scale set by the printer's union. But since females were not allowed into the union and couldn't become real printers, Angie and Pattie considered the job only temporary, a way to earn pin money.

To Angie, Pattie, and Addie, living in a bustling community of three thousand people that covered two whole square miles was way more exciting than their former dull mining camps. When young men flocked to the Hutchinsons' doorstep, Sarah invited them into the house so that she could keep an eye on them. If Charlie Donofrio and his violin happened to be in the crowd, furniture was pushed aside for square dancing.

Donofrio's Ice Cream Parlor on Washington Street soon became a favorite gathering place for Angie's group after church on Sundays. These teenagers included Pattie, Addie, Bob and George Linville, Charles and Frank Tweed, and the Etter and Dorris boys.

One Sunday, George Linville came up with the idea of infiltrating a Salvation Army camp meeting. Angie recollected what happened out of his suggestion.

> **Young people do some queer things, not for meanness, but just to have something to do. There wasn't much for young people to do outside of the Good Templars and some of the close church organizations.**
>
> **Our group enjoyed the Salvation Army Camp meetings and thought their prolonged "A-a—men's" and "Praise God's" were funny. We laughed and joined in as we winked at each other.**
>
> **We dared George Linville to go up to the Mourner's Bench. He did, keeping his face toward us and winking once in a while. We laughed ourselves almost into hysterics at George.**
>
> **[Each Sunday] George was at the Mourner's Bench until we didn't think it was funny any more and stopped going so often. When we did go again, there was George. He stayed with the Salvation Army, for which I have held him in high esteem and deplored the discourtesy and ignorance of the rest of us.**
>
> **George had been a little on the wild side and confided to my mother that his mother had predicted the end of a rope for him unless he mended his ways.**

When the territorial capital moved to Phoenix in 1889, the newlyweds, Gen and J. K. Murphy, took up residence in Phoenix because J.K. worked out of the sheriff's office that was located in the capitol. His staff included Henry King, J.K.'s cousin and a frequent visitor at the Hutchinson social center.

On one such visit, Henry kept staring at the black and green stripes on Angie's skirt. "Angie, I'll give you a whole dollar for one of those stripes," he said.

Never one to shrink from a dare, Angie handed him the scissors and let him cut a vertical stripe from her skirt right in front of her horrified mother. She wrote of the incident,

**Mother and Father were not in the least amused, but everyone else thought it was funny. I went into another room to sew up my skirt and later bought twelve yards of challis with the dollar Henry gave me.**

A few days later, while visiting at Gen's, Addie came flying out of the house. "Get the hoe! There's a snake in the house!"

Angie rushed in with a hoe. There, coiled behind a lounge, was the biggest snake she had ever seen, with its red tongue flicking out at her. Up to her ears in adrenalin, she pounded the snake with all her might before discovering it was the stripe from her dress. Angie wasn't the only one to fall into Henry King's snake trap. J.K. reported that his cousin had also terrorized the capitol with the stripe from her dress.

## My Maw Will Fire You

As the family scholar, Angie had long known she was destined to become a schoolteacher. Pattie remained at the *Republican*, but Angie quit working to enroll in Miss Clara A. Evans's Teacher Training School. Rather than actual training for the classroom, Miss Evans stuffed students' heads with the information needed to pass an examination for teacher certification. It took Angie only a few months.

She began looking for a teaching position in 1889, the same year that propaganda from the American Protective Association was circulating throughout the country under the guise of patriotism. Since many immigrants to this country were Catholic, the APA's chief aim was to place the government into the hands of Protestants and keep Catholic teachers out of public schools. This secret and oath-bound order operated clandestinely in much the same manner as the Ku Klux Klan. Handbills denouncing Catholics appeared all over the streets of Phoenix, and public schools began looking closely at the religious affiliation of their teachers.

Angie dreaded writing the word "Catholic" on her teaching applications, but she could not lie about her faith. Consequently, not a single school in the Phoenix area responded to her applications.

However, Maricopa County's new School District Number Nine, covering the little settlements of Wickenburg, Vulture City, and Seymour, had more serious concerns than religious affiliation. Teachers didn't remain long at these isolated schools with poor accommodations. Twenty-year-old Angie got the nod from the Wickenburg School Board for the 1889 to 1890 school year.

Wickenburg's former glory days had evaporated with the closing of the Vulture Mine and surrounding stamp mills. Angie found it to be almost a ghost town now. Commercial buildings and once-lovely adobe homes, mud stained and crumbling, stood abandoned and forlorn. The town's few remaining residents still catered to freighters stopping for supplies, meals, and lodging on their way to or from Ehrenberg, Prescott, or Phoenix. Along with a number of Hispanic farmers who cultivated subsistence crops along the Hassayampa's bottomlands, Henry Wickenburg and Frederick Brill had more substantial spreads.

There were but four Anglo women in the whole town — Mrs. Tompkins, the wife of the mail carrier; Mrs. Bacon, whose husband was a trustee of the school; Kate Henderson, soon to be Angie's roommate; and Mrs. Egloff, a board trustee along with Henry Wickenburg and Mr. Bacon. These four women welcomed Angie into their small sisterhood, not caring about her religious affiliation.

Minnie Egloff had three children and ran a boardinghouse, a general store, and the post office on Center Street in addition to fulfilling her duties on the school board. Angie described her as a kind, tiny, live wire of a woman and her husband, Jack, as a tall, slender man with a dark brown beard and hair to match. He ran the saloon end of the business when he wasn't shooting jackrabbits or making sauerkraut in ten-gallon kegs from the cabbage in Henry Wickenburg's garden.

In describing the Egloff establishment, Angie wrote that a wide porch ran across the rear of the old one-story main adobe house. This porch contained washtubs, benches, and canvas cots that could be rented for twenty-five cents a night. Additional rooms were available along the front of the main building, some with real walls and doors and others with nothing more than burlap par-

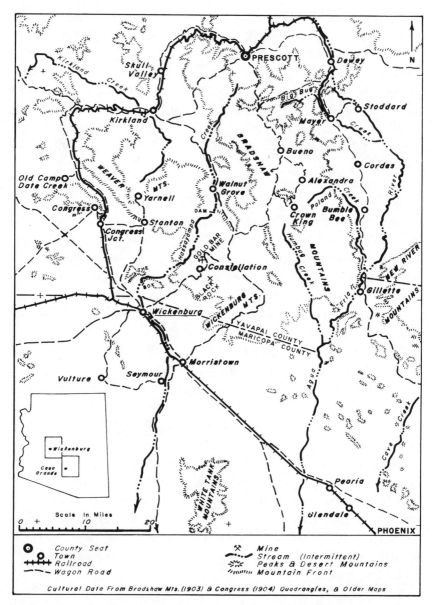

Portions of Maricopa and Yavapai Counties showing areas around Wickenburg, 1902. (Map by Donald F. Hammer, modified from U.S. government maps dated 1903 and older)

titions to divide them. Rugs covered dirt floors, and each room contained the standard washstand, pitcher, and slop jar. Nails provided the only means of keeping a traveler's garments off the floor. These fine accommodations could be procured for a dollar a night.

Angie took room and board with Minnie Egloff in a seven-by-nine-foot room overlooking the horse corrals. She shared this updated facility with Kate Henderson, whom she described as a fine-looking woman with golden hair and fair skin. The area's cattlemen and miners called Kate "the starry-eyed enchantress of the Hassayampa" because she had tiny, white growths close to the pupil of each eye that caused her eyes to twinkle.

Each night Kate would tightly close the room's one window to keep out the flies and odor. Come morning, the room would be so depleted of oxygen its one window would be opened to cold air while the two women shivered through their bathing rituals.

After Angie settled into the Egloff boardinghouse, she, Kate, Mrs. Egloff, and the Egloffs' three children set out to check on the condition of the schoolhouse. With little in the way of funds, the Wickenburg School rented the former home of George and Molly Monroe for seven dollars a month. A cursory inspection found the building's front door off its hinges and the house filled with accumulated filth and debris. It took a whole day of shoveling, sweeping, mopping, and washing down benches and tables to ready the school for its opening.

Angie took one last glance at the orderly classroom before moving the door back onto its frame. As she picked up the door, a rattlesnake took issue at this invasion of its privacy. In no time, the Egloff children, screaming with delight, bombarded the coiled snake with rocks. Eleven-year-old Jimmie Egloff carried the dead rattler off to the bushes, and Angie didn't give the incident another thought.

On the first day of school, the snake reappeared to greet each girl entering the schoolyard. Eleven-year-old Jimmy Egloff merrily chased his prey around the building with the snake draped across a stick, its rattles shaking ominously. He paid no heed to Angie's commands to drop the snake.

Finally, Angie managed to ambush Jimmy from the other direction with a switch in her hand. As he reluctantly dropped the snake, he loudly proclaimed that he would have Miss Angela fired. "My maw's on the school board, an' she tole me she'd fire any teacher who so much as lays a hand on me."

Though Minnie Egloff had warned about her son's hot temper, nothing could have prepared Angie for his physical assault after school one evening. The boy gouged his hand on a nail holding the door in place. Blaming Angie, he came at her with eyes blazing and fists flailing. Angie held her ground and grabbed both of Jimmy's wrists, pushed up close, and tripped him backward with her leg. They fell to the ground with Angie on top. Although the boy was larger, Angie managed to keep him pinned to the ground until he quit struggling and screaming. He began to cry, "I'm sorry, Miss Angela. I'll be a good boy from now on."

Jimmy lived up to his promise, became one of Angie's most dependable students, and helped her keep an eye on the primary tots.

She had about forty children of all ages, mostly Hispanic, from five-year-olds to Tiburcio Villa, a hard-working lad of twenty-one. Like Laura Copeland's young stepson, Fred Brill Jr., most of these students came from farms and camps along the river. Angie worked with the primary class for an hour or so each morning, then turned them out into an enclosed yard to play with whatever objects she could find. She watched the little ones through a window that faced the play yard while she taught the older students from books she had brought from home. Other than a blackboard, her only teaching tool was a primary chart for the youngsters; she had nothing for the older students until she talked the school board into buying an astronomical chart.

## A Warehouse Becomes a Morgue

In 1890, it rained all during the month of January. Every glimpse of the sun caused rejoicing among the students. By February, the sun was but a distant memory as sievelike clouds continued pouring water onto already saturated ground. The waters of the Hassayampa generally flowed beneath the sand-filled streambed, with an occasional shallow pool showing above the surface. But when this river began overflowing its banks, the denizens of Wickenburg began to worry about the stability of the Walnut Grove Dam lying thirty miles upstream. It impounded a fifty-foot-deep lake halfway between Prescott and Wickenburg, fed by snowmelt from the Bradshaw Mountains. Angie wrote about the residents' concern.

**The dam's builders claimed it to be the largest structure of solid concrete in the United States at that time, but some said the builders had cut corners by**

**using rock fill, instead of concrete, and that the dam didn't even rest on solid bedrock. If the dam should give way, the raging Hassayampa waters would wipe out the town of Wickenburg. The Egloff place, right on the bank of the river, would surely be the first to go.**

Reports came in that the dam showed signs of weakening, but Wickenburg residents were assured that if a break seemed imminent, fast couriers would be sent with the warning. Despite this assurance, Angie and Kate took turns keeping watch every night for almost a month.

On the night before Washington's Birthday, a school holiday, Angie told Kate, "We can't keep this up forever. I'm exhausted and need a good night's sleep."

She slept right through the disaster that brought an eighty-foot wall of water down the Hassayampa when the lower dam gave way during the night. This deluge was restricted by a narrow box canyon above Wickenburg that held back the flow of floodwater and permitted it to spread out to moderate depth and velocity across the flatter land of the town. A geographic miracle had saved Wickenburg.

Before daylight Kate shook Angie awake. "Get up quick! The dam's gone out!"

An incredulous Angie looked out the window to see that the Egloff buildings stood on a peninsula of higher ground with floodwater on three sides, filling both the privy and the well. She shuddered at the thought of this typhoid potential.

Brown floodwater swirled down the wash on Tegner Street, as Kate and Angie made their way toward the bank of the river. No sound but the lapping of water broke the eerie silence, no sign of life, not even a bird or a cricket. Dead animals, fencing, roofs, and broken wagon parts bobbed up and down in the water around debris-laden mesquite and ironwood trees, testifying to the flood's height and savagery. Something in a nearby catclaw bush caught their attention. Upon closer inspection, they found it to be the queue, or braid, of a Chinese man. They looked at each other in horror, trying to digest the enormity of what this discovery portended.

By noon, a warehouse on Front Street had been turned into a morgue. Not a shred of clothing remained on the bodies brought in by searchers. These bodies were covered and laid in rows on the floor as the death toll mounted. An ear, a foot, and the queue awaited their owners.

Over the next few days, forty-six bodies lined the floor, and according to rough estimates, over a hundred people had disappeared. Because of the need to feed all the searchers, the town began running out of food. Henry Wickenburg's garden, a former reliable source of produce, lay buried under tons of silt, so Jack Egloff broke out his barrels of sauerkraut.

As men fashioned crude caskets of mesquite or wood salvaged from the flood, Angie and Kate prepared the sand-covered bodies of the women for burial. They left for last a Chinese woman, whose very long hair filled with sand and weeds looked formidable. During life, her hair had been tied at intervals and worn in puffs. Kate sobbed as they anchored it in place with long hairpins. Angie tried to remain resolute, but the lump in her throat turned to tears when Sarah and William appeared with a search party, fearing their daughter had been washed away in the flood. Her parents carried with them the body of a young girl found on top of a displaced boulder on their way into Wickenburg. After helping with the interment, William and Sarah returned to Phoenix.

Meanwhile, word reached Wickenburg that people in ranches and camps upriver were stranded without food. Angie and Kate volunteered to take supplies to the Roark Ranch, a ten-mile ride on horseback, accompanied by two cowboy friends, George Warren and Bill Clore.

The foursome arrived at the ranch midday, just in time to help shovel silt out of the main house. After this exhausting activity, no one could face the return trip. They would spend the night at the ranch and get a fresh start in the morning. George and Bill cooked an evening meal of jerky gravy and biscuits baked in a Dutch oven with campfire coals.

Getting an early start the next morning, the rescue party decided to check on another camp on the way back to Wickenburg, but with all the trails and familiar landmarks washed out, they wandered in and out of thickets for hours. By late afternoon Angie's posterior discomfort had become unbearable, and she begged for a time-out. They dismounted, built a campfire, and stretched out beside it for a short nap. Darkness fell on the snoozing foursome. Between alternate bouts of freezing and roasting, the short siesta became an all-night nap.

Stiff and sore the next morning, with blisters in all the wrong places, Angie and Kate declared they would walk into town. The cowboys objected to this lack of class, padded the girls' saddles, and coaxed them back on their mounts.

These two young ladies and their escorts rode innocently into town, expecting to be hailed as good Samaritans. Instead, they were castigated roundly from all sides for having spent two nights alone with the men.

Jack Egloff scolded, "I'll spank you both to an inch of your lives if you ever do such a foolhardy thing again while you're under my roof." He turned to Angie. "And you, of all people! What kind of example does this behavior set for your students?"

Mrs. Egloff came to their defense. "Knowing you girls and Bill and George as I do, nothing the gossips can say will make me believe anything bad about either of you."

"Even the bushes are talking," wrote Pattie from Phoenix. "Angie, why do you always plunge into these situations without considering the consequences?"

### An Expert Chirographer

At the end of the 1890 school year, Angie returned to her family in Phoenix to find the town undergoing flooding problems of its own. Floodwater from the swollen Salt River cut diagonally across Central Avenue at Washington Street, reducing many of the buildings in its path to piles of adobe mud. Fortunately, the Hutchinson home had been spared, and Angie found her family providing shelter to Gen, J.K., and numerous other friends and relatives.

Pattie, now an expert typesetter, had taken a job at the *Phoenix Evening Gazette*, a Democratic paper and rival of the *Phoenix Republican*. "Why don't you apply for a summer job, Angie? My editor, J. O. Dunbar, will jump at the chance to hire you because literate, sober typesetters are hard to come by."

Angie wrote about her summer experience with J. O. Dunbar.

**In time I became a very good compositor as far as clean (error-free) proofs were concerned, but I never did reach the speed of Pattie and the other girls. Owing to my clean proofs, I got a lot of J.O.'s editorials. One had to be an expert chirographer to be able to read them. He wrote in light, wiggling lines, with only the first and final letters legible.**

**J.O. was a colorful writer and prided himself on his spelling. Once I had a run-in with him about the spelling of the word "incalculable." He always left off the last "l," and I always put it in. One day, in an irate frame of mind, he came**

**after me for correcting his spelling. I showed him the word in the dictionary, and he couldn't believe he'd been misspelling it for the last forty years.**

J.O.'s printers belonged to the Typographer's Union and were threatening to strike for higher wages. Angie and Pattie realized that they worked at a disadvantage, but they were in no position to question any established practice. Apparently, regular printers were paid for the time it took to disassemble type and distribute it into trays, but the girls were paid only by the measurement of their proofs. Angie wrote about the practice.

**We had to throw in [sort] all of the type we set up, and the six-point [smallest type] was divided between us. We didn't get anything for the distribution [putting type back into alphabetical trays]. If we didn't distribute the type ourselves, we wouldn't have any to set up for our strings [columns]. Our strings consisted of proofs of the type we had set. These strings were pasted together [put end to end] and measured for inches. When we set six point, called *non pareil*, we were allowed to double it, that is, we could cut the column proof down the middle and paste the two parts end to end for measurement.**

Angie and Pattie couldn't understand why the printers scowled at them, calling them "rats and scabs" under their breath. In reality, the girls worked for half of what the printers were paid as members of the Typographer's Union.

Whether these printers remained in the employ of J.O. is not known, but if they quit, that might explain why Angie remained at the *Gazette* instead of returning to the classroom in the autumn of 1891. She had great affection for J. O. Dunbar.

## To Cushion an Ego

Perhaps tired of typesetting by this time, Angie returned to the classroom for the 1892 to 1893 school year. She took a position at the tiny Enterprise School, thirteen miles north of Gila Bend. This school served a small, isolated, agricultural settlement on the Gila River that had once been a stage stop on the old Gila Trail.

On a good day, twenty-five students might show up for school, but normally only ten to twelve students attended. The bulk of these students, five of them, came from the Cooper family and challenged Angie's diplomatic teaching skills. Eighteen-year-old George Cooper, whom Angie assessed as being not as mentally quick as his younger brothers and sisters, led the group. He carried his head to one side as if to say, "See, I told you so," and his siblings believed everything he said to be God's truth.

Between George and his youngest brother, Princey, Angie had her hands full. Princey had convinced himself that he was different from other "mere mortals" because he had fallen into a canal and almost drowned. He told Angie he couldn't understand why he was being rolled on a barrel when he regained consciousness. Angie tried to explain how this procedure had restored his respiration, but Princey didn't want to hear it. He preferred to tell his classmates that he alone knew the secrets of the other side.

Angie had given the students homework in their physical geography book, a chapter about clouds. When the students stood in line to be quizzed about their assignment, George was first.

"What are clouds made of?" Angie asked.

He answered, "Clouds are made of smoke."

"Next."

"Clouds are made of smoke," said George's sister.

On down the line, each student echoed George, a unanimous declaration that clouds were made of smoke.

Angie said to them, "Children, I'm sure you did not study your lesson. I want you to take your books home tonight and come back with the correct answer tomorrow."

The next day, George Cooper again stood at the head of the line. He declared, "My dad says that the publishers of our geography book are ignorant. He can prove that clouds are made of smoke."

"And how can he do this?" asked Angie.

"Because every time my dad burns brush or stubble in the field, great clouds of smoke go up into the sky and return as rain."

This answer called for great diplomacy. "Well, that's news to me. Suppose we make some kind of test to prove what clouds are made of? I want each of you to bring in a fruit jar tomorrow. We'll gather smoke in them and let the jars stand overnight. If we find water, I'll join your opinion that the textbook is wrong."

The next day, Angie and her children built a fire of the smokiest material they could find, filled the jars with the thick, black smoke, and fastened the tops tightly. The following morning, the students found to their chagrin, that the jars were coated with thick, black smut.

"My stars!" Angie exclaimed. "Here we expected to find water instead of smut. Our geography book must be correct, after all!"

Angie's surprised response helped cushion George's ego. He came away from the lesson thinking that his teacher had learned something along with the rest of them.


### Hargrave Sets Up Suitors

Enterprise teachers always boarded at the Hargrave Ranch. Angie wrote that Mr. Hargrave was a friendly man who liked to tease his wife and their boarders. Angie laughed off this teasing until the day, early in the school year, that Mrs. Hargrave took her aside. "Miss Angie, I don't want you to take this personally, but—but maybe you could find somewhere else to live?"

Taken aback, Angie asked if she had done something to offend her hosts.

"No, you are a perfectly nice young lady—just like all the rest," Mrs. Hargrave stammered. "But all the young ladies who stay here have brought me sorrow. You see, my husband, he's—he's—too—."

Angie finished Mrs. Hargrave's thought. "He's too attentive? Is that it?"

Mrs. Hargrave nodded woefully.

Angie tried to explain that she was sure Mr. Hargrave had the best of intentions. Under no circumstances would Angie be alone with Mrs. Hargrave's husband.

Mrs. Hargrave reluctantly agreed that Angie could remain at the ranch, but she tested her young boarder in various ways. Angie wrote,

> **If the three of us were sitting around the fireplace in the evening, Mrs. Hargrave would sometimes go to her room without saying a word. That was my cue to excuse myself and go to my room, too. Sometimes she tried to leave her husband alone at the ranch with me, but I always protested and went along with her on errands.**
>
> **Hargrave was a very decent sort of man, and if his wife could ever learn to trust him fully, she would be very happy.**

However, Mrs. Hargrave did learn to trust Angie, and the two women developed a strong affectionate bond. Angie and the Hargraves' son, Pascal, rode to school in a two-wheeled cart each morning, carrying lunches Mrs. Hargrave packed with slabs of immense fried yams that had been grown on the ranch. They returned in the evening to find cold watermelon with two spoons awaiting them on the porch. Each Saturday, Mrs. Hargrave baked a special lemon pie for Angie. While she spoiled her boarder, Mr. Hargrave worked on his matchmaking skills.

It was almost Christmas break when Hargrave began pitting two lonely bachelors against each other. Dunn was his hired hand, and Murdiss, a tenant, lived in a little shack on the ranch. Hargrave told each of them separately, "You have an excellent chance with Miss Angela. All you have to do is speak up and let her know how you feel."

When Angie left to spend Christmas in Phoenix, Hargrave challenged the timid Murdiss. "Are you going to let Dunn get that schoolmarm without making any effort to beat him to it?"

Murdiss answered, "You just wait until that gal gets back from Phoenix. I'm making my move then."

When Angie returned from Phoenix after Christmas, she expected Mr. Hargrave to meet her at Gila Bend in his comfortable light spring wagon to take her to the ranch. Instead, she found Murdiss waiting for her and almost laughed out loud when she saw him outfitted in a gaily patterned shirt, a bright red necktie, and green gloves. Thinking that Hargrave had sent Murdiss, she climbed aboard the high seat of his wagon, exposed to the icy air and not looking forward to a trip with this curious fellow.

Right off, Murdiss began telling her all about himself, how he kept his private affairs strictly to himself, that while he rented the shack on Hargrave's place, he was not a common laborer. "Nobody knows what a wonderful life I could give a woman or how much money I have in the bank."

Angie detected the odor of alcohol on his breath and was beginning to worry when she saw the Hargrave team approaching. But it wasn't Mr. Hargrave driving the spring wagon; it was Dunn.

Both teams stopped in the middle of the road. Right off, Dunn demanded to know why Angie didn't wait for the Hargrave wagon, whereupon Murdiss jumped down from his wagon and berated Dunn for interfering in his affairs. Angie had to take a choice between the two. She chose Dunn for no reason other than the Hargrave wagon was more comfortable. This enraged Murdiss and, no doubt, encouraged Dunn to think that she preferred him.

When Angie later told Hargrave about the near duel on the roadside, he smiled knowingly and began planning even more skullduggery.

First he contrived a reason to send Dunn, his hired hand, to a neighboring farm on foot. Before Dunn left, Hargrave warned him, "Watch your back. Murdiss is plenty pissed at you and might be laying for you with a gun."

Then that ornery Hargrave hid in some bushes midway, waited for Dunn to pass, then fired his pistol into the air. Of course, that put Dunn into a panic.

The upshot to this affair came when Hargrave discovered that Murdiss had disappeared without telling anyone good-bye. Hargrave questioned Dunn about it.

Dunn shrugged his shoulders, trying to look wide eyed and innocent. "I dunno what happened to Murdiss. After he tried to kill me, I guess he got scared and ran away. I didn't do anything to him."

## Blowflies Become Screwworms

Angie interacted with the families of her students, often being invited to meals and other occasions in their homes. She liked the Wadleigh family and occasionally walked home with Virgil and Sylvia Wadleigh to stop in for a chat with their mother. Angie described Mrs. Wadleigh:

> **Large cottonwood trees shaded their home and presented a rather artistic appearance, which seemed appropriate to the activities of Mrs. Wadleigh, who painted some of the most beautiful pictures of wildlife and scenes of a land far distant from our desert environment. Mrs. Wadleigh, who had dark, softly curling hair that seldom felt the pull of a comb, was almost a work of art herself. There was something about her appearance and language that bespoke better times than the family was presently undergoing. She was intensely proud and tried in every possible way to hide their poverty.**
>
> **Besides painting she spent much time with her baby chicks which brought in an occasional dollar or two and helped the family larder. Her poultry house was situated under a large cottonwood tree. The roof was made of brush, and the place was almost buried under the fallen leaves of several seasons.**

One morning on the way to school, Angie and Pascal heard Virgil calling, "Come quick! My mother's hurt!"

As they drew closer to the house, they could hear agonizing screams coming from inside. With a pounding heart, Angie entered the house to find Mr. Wadleigh daubing lard and flour on his wife's charred back with his own badly scorched hands. He looked up woefully. "The children were playing in the yard with matches and accidentally ignited the brush roof of the chicken house. My missus rushed in to save a setting of eggs, and the blazing roof fell on her back. I tried to stop her, but she was too quick for me. Her whole back was in flames by the time I dragged her out and got her rolled in a blanket. Will you get Mr. Hargrave to go for a doctor in Gila Bend?"

After sending Pascal home to ask his parents to dismiss school and get a doctor, Angie took over just as if she knew what she was doing. She rummaged through trunks and cupboards, looking for any clean material that could be used as dressings for the burns.

After examining the wounds, the doctor gave a rather dire prognosis along with directions for Mrs. Wadleigh's care. "Given such a large, deep burn area, this could easily become fatal. It will take the most assiduous care to pull her through. Her dressings must be changed twice daily and thrown into the fireplace for disposal. You must be very careful about handling these dressings."

Angie and Mrs. Hargrave took turns changing Mrs. Wadleigh's bandages. Hundreds of pounds of clean, white rags came in from Phoenix and Gila Bend in response to Angie's pleas. Dead flesh sloughed off Mrs. Wadleigh's back for a month before her condition began to improve. At this point, Mr. Wadleigh told the women that he would take over their nursing chores. Still, both Angie and Mrs. Hargrave dropped in to check on Mrs. Wadleigh's progress.

On one visit, Mr. Wadleigh answered the door with tears in his eyes, saying to Angie, "I'm a failure as a nurse! I've let blowflies get under the dressings, and now there's screwworms burrowing into her flesh."

Angie tried to reassure him. "This is no reflection on your care. One fly can do a lot of damage, and without screens on your windows and doors, there's no way to prevent them from getting in. We'd better get the doctor out here again."

The doctor demonstrated how the wormholes could be detected by running water over the sores and noting where little bubbles appeared. Medicine was then injected into the holes.

Mrs. Wadleigh recovered, but her badly damaged upper left arm remained as bone with skin drawn over it. With perseverance, she learned to use this arm quite well.

Angie's days in Enterprise were like living in a large family. Here, she needed to be all things to all people and had little time to herself. Even Sundays required that she be at the schoolhouse for Bible study, but she would never forget the leaderless discussions held there. She described those days:

**A Bible verse was selected and people took turns telling how they interpreted it. The most interesting interpretations came from a Chinese farmer by the name of Lee. Our little nondenominational group came closer to the spirit of true Christian love than anything I've ever experienced.**

She returned to Phoenix at the end of the school year, and not long after, a letter came in the mail:

Dear Miss Angie,
    This is to let you no I wud like to marry you. I wud make you a good husband. I wud cut all the wood and carry in all the water and help you all I cud around the house. I wud get you a school and it wud be a good school too. Plese rite and let me no and I will cum for you at wunst.

Sincerely,
Dunn

Angie wrote back to tell Dunn that, although she was flattered by his proposal, she planned to teach in Wickenburg the following school year. She couldn't continue teaching if she were to marry.

## Decent Girls Sit Sideways

Returning to her old school in Wickenburg for the 1894 to 1895 school year, Angie found the town still struggling to overcome the effects of the flood. Farming and mining activity had come almost to a standstill. Strangely, she wrote nothing about where she boarded or her teaching conditions. However, she did tell in great detail about several adventures that had nothing to do with school.

The first adventure took place one bright Saturday morning when Jennie Tompkins, the daughter of the mail carrier, asked Angie to help make a twenty-four-mile mail run into Vulture City. Jennie's father, too sick to carry the mail, still managed to ready his two-wheeled, sulky-style cart for the girls. He tied water canteens on Brownie, a huge horse that made the cart look like a play toy by comparison. With no floor to the sulky, the girls used the mailbags as a footrest.

Once under way, after traveling for an hour or so, they heard a crunching sound under the cart and found that the bow of the right shaft had fallen between the spokes of the wheel. Before they could stop, the same thing happened to the left shaft. Brownie stopped of his own accord and stayed put to await further orders.

The girls held a hurried conversation about whether they should return to Wickenburg or ride the horse into Vulture City. Angie said she thought she could see the divide, a high point between Wickenburg and the mine, so they must already be halfway there. After they had convinced themselves to go on, Jennie threw the harness across Brownie's back, somehow fastened it, and tied on the mailbags and canteens of water. Then the girls climbed aboard Brownie, using the cart as a platform.

Society decreed many "thou shall not's" for young ladies and women, and one of these was the impropriety of sitting astride a horse. True to their upbringing, the girls sat sideways with Jennie's feet pointing one direction and Angie's the other. Angie held onto Jennie as she tried to balance herself behind on the hard straps. Jennie's seating was none too substantial either, so the girls swayed from side to side each time Brownie took a step. They began to giggle, and the more they giggled, the less they concentrated on balance. Angie slid backward, heels over head into a soft sand wash. Again Brownie, with great intelligence and patience, stopped and looked around inquiringly. Angie waited until their spasms of laughter subsided before she climbed back aboard Brownie.

In due time, this gaiety turned to worry, for they had expected to see Vulture Peak before now. Time and again, when they thought they spotted the landmark in the distance, they would round a hill only to see another just like it in the distance. By the time they reached the old company office at Vulture, the afternoon sun cast long shadows on the ground.

The girls found their legs trembling from muscle fatigue and hunger when they finally slid off Brownie and gave the mailbags to a grouchy old assayer in charge of the office. "Our sulky broke down and we've traveled all day without food," Angie told him. "Do you have anything we might eat?"

The old assayer treated the girls to a stony glare and a lecture about attempting such a journey alone. "Besides," he said, "I'm not prepared to serve meals to transients."

Throwing pride aside, the girls begged for food so pitifully that the grouch finally opened a can of stewed tomatoes and gave them two spoons along with a package of soda crackers.

Somewhat fortified by these rations, the girls then asked if he knew where they might rent a buggy or some kind of vehicle for the trip home. The assayer shook his head. "I'm sorry, but there's nothing available around here. You'll have to go back on your horse, but if I were you, I'd get astride him. It's foolish and dangerous to ride sideways." Thus saying, he tied his Vulture City mailbags onto Brownie and went into his office, slamming the door behind him.

Our young ladies had no choice but to climb onto Brownie's bare back, take their former positions, and ride off indignantly. Night birds and bats flew overhead. When they reached Vulture Peak, Angie nudged Jenny. "You know, maybe we should take that ungracious man's advice and straddle the horse. It's too dark for anyone to see us now."

Brownie waited for the rearrangement, then plodded on to the accompaniment of rattling canteens and the clinking of harness chains. His hooves tapped out hollow sounds over underground gypsum deposits. Hours passed. Realizing they wouldn't get home much before sunup, the girls wondered aloud how Jennie's father would react to their delayed arrival.

About midnight, Angie and Jennie heard riders approaching. Jennie reined Brownie behind some bushes at the side of the road. "Shhh. We better not take any chances. It might be bandits coming after the mail from the mine."

Brownie neighed to the oncoming horses, and soon they found themselves surrounded by fifteen range riders, a search party dispatched by Jennie's father. The men took turns berating the girls for their foolishness, calling them numbskulls and idiots for not turning back when their cart broke down only four miles out of Wickenburg.

Angie and Jennie knew it was useless to explain that they thought it was their patriotic duty to carry the mail to Vulture City.

### Just Pull the Signal Cord

For years Angie had listened to tales of the marvelous underground caverns at the Vulture Mine. A hundred-foot tunnel between two inclined shafts purportedly led to a huge chamber supported by pillars of rich gold ore. This chamber was said to open into stalagmite and stalactite caves haunted by the ghosts of dead miners.

Since the mine hadn't been in production for the last few years, only a caretaker watched the premises. This caretaker, Jim Hammond, became the ladies' escort on the day that Angie, Kate, Laura Brill, and an unidentified woman decided to pay a nostalgic visit to the site of old Vulture City.

The women had obviously made the decision on impulse, perhaps after church, since they were all dressed in their Sunday finery. Kate wore a lace hat covered with roses, Laura, a lovely China silk dress, and Angie, a white cashmere sweater trimmed in black velvet. They had managed to procure a wagon and a driver, who sat in the shade while the ladies revisited the sites of Kirkland's store, the Chinese restaurant, Dr. Osborn's home, and Angie's home, long obscured by mill tailings.

Jim Hammond invited the women to trudge up a hill to once again marvel at the huge flywheel in the hoisting works that had raised the rich gold ores to the surface through an inclined shaft. Angie and Laura wondered out loud, as they had so many times in the past, how such a monstrous piece of machinery could have been freighted up the Colorado River and carted by mule team across the Mohave Desert.

Jim Hammond had once been the mine's hoisting engineer, so he expertly led the ladies to the top of the inclined shaft and began spinning his web of entrapment. "No human can believe the beauty of those huge chambers of crystal that lie below. Someday it will rival Mammoth Cave. My company is getting ready to dismantle all machinery and stop work entirely. This may be the only chance you'll ever have to go belowground." He beckoned toward an ore skip at the collar of the shaft. "Hop aboard, Ladies, for the thrill of a lifetime!"

Due to a widely held superstition that feminine presence belowground brought bad luck to miners, Angie had never been allowed below the surface of a mine. Without hesitation, she crawled into the dirty, slanting ore skip and positioned herself on the top edge where it attached to the cable. "Let's go!"

Carefully, the others spread out pieces of canvas that Jim thoughtfully provided for dress protection and wedged themselves into the remaining space. Jim handed each of them a tallow candle. "Just pull the cord three times if you want to come up. There's nothing to worry about."

As the ore skip descended into the dark shaft, the air became increasingly stale. Kate, feeling a little woozy, got disoriented, held her candle too close to her lace hat, and set it ablaze. Fumbling momentarily with a long hairpin, her skipmates ripped the hat from her head and sent it overboard. Kate only quit crying over her singed hair and ruined hat long enough to throw up over the side of the skip. Laura gave the signal cord three sharp tugs. Nothing happened. Angrily, Laura yanked the cord again. In response, the ore car picked up more speed in its descent. Its occupants screamed, cried, and cursed.

Abruptly, the skip halted, swinging in midair as if the hoist operator couldn't make up his mind whether to send it up or down. Hammond couldn't resist. He sent the skip plunging downward into the icy sump at the bottom of the shaft, a move calculated to soak shoes, stockings, petticoats, and dresses. The ladies gasped in shock when they hit the subterranean water. Then, as the ladies shivered, the skip slowly began its ascent.

Jim Hammond realized it wouldn't be in his best interest to bring the ladies up to the surface, so he stopped the skip at an adit, a horizontal entry to the shaft. Thankful to see a thin ray of sunlight at the far end of the tunnel, the women piled out of the car without a moment's hesitation. Slumbering cave bats and pack rats startled awake at the sound of laborious breathing and tumbling rocks, but no chambers of wondrous crystals appeared along the way. If the ghosts of dead miners happened to be watching, they would have laughed at the fate of these female intruders crawling along the sacred corridor on hands and knees.

Four hardly recognizable, mud-encrusted figures unfolded themselves into blessed sunlight at the mouth of the tunnel. They sat for a spell, nursing bleeding knees before tackling the tortuous trail up to the hoisting works. Each agonizing step brought them closer to the havoc they would soon inflict on Jim Hammond . . . or so they thought.

Jim Hammond had vanished!

The driver's face reflected a mixture of concern, puzzlement, and mirth when the four once-lovely ladies lifted their ragged skirts to climb aboard his wagon. "What happened to your beautiful hat?" he asked Kate.

"It's in the bottom of the Vulture Mine," she answered through gritted teeth. "I'm bringing back a posse to send Jim Hammond down to get it."

William Tallentyre
Hutchinson, born in
Pennsylvania in 1834,
married Sarah Higgins at
Virginia City, Nevada, in
1864.

### The Hanging Rock Ledge

After the close of school in 1895, Angie found her father and J. K. Murphy
packing an outfit to do some mining in the Black Hills north of Wickenburg,
where they had staked claims and already established a camp. William invited
Angie and Addie to tag along if they wanted. "We'll even give you the honor of
picking out a place to start our first adit, but you'll have to ride muleback since
our wagon is full of gear. It's a pretty rough twelve-mile trip from Wickenburg."

Regardless of whether Angie and Addie sat sideways or astride, a mule's
rounded haunches doesn't provide a particularly comfortable ride. Our two-
some made it into camp, where their sore backsides were given a day or two
of rest before again mounting mules to begin the big assignment of locating
the right place to begin digging.

William may have already known about the "hanging ledge" of quartz rock
with its visible gold vein, or the young ladies may have found it themselves.
Either way, when they came upon this magnificent ledge, they knew instinc-

tively that this was the right place to begin tunneling. They excitedly piled up rocks to mark the spot.

Addie couldn't wait to carry the good news back to camp and took off immediately. Angie's slower mule couldn't catch up, and suddenly none of the terrain looked familiar. Although Angie thought she was heading in the right direction, the mule wanted to go a different way. No matter how hard she kicked his flanks, yelled at him, and told him he was crazy, he refused to budge. Finally, remembering the old adage about letting a mule have its head, she gave in and let him go where he wanted, which, of course, was right back to camp. That evening, Angie gave her mule an extra helping of oats and confided her newfound respect for him and his relatives.

After leading William and J.K. to the hanging ledge, the two proud ladies basked in the men's lavish praise for their good eyes and prospecting instincts. Picks hit the ground in their chosen spot. J.K. swore this gold mine would rival the Vulture.

Eastern gold seekers often scoured mining districts, hoping to snag a likely looking prospect in the bud. When William and J.K. had drifted along the vein for about 125 feet, some strangers from Minnesota arrived in camp. Greatly impressed with the quartz ledge and its visible gold, they began negotiations to buy the claim, proposing the development of a Black Rock Company funded by eastern capital.

Knowing they would be hard-pressed to develop their prospect alone, William and J.K. readily agreed to a cash down payment with the balance to be paid in Black Rock Company stock. J.K. agreed to remain in camp to oversee the mine's development. Gen came from Phoenix, and the couple took up quarters in a tent house.

The strangers from Minnesota did an excellent job of promoting the Black Rock Company. People with high expectations poured in from Duluth and Superior, Minnesota. Company buildings, a mess hall, and boardinghouses turned the camp into a bustling center of activity, a place where dreams of wealth would be realized.

Gen watched all these developments in amazement, writing to the family that the company seemed to squander money needlessly, while promoters continued to use Angie and Addie's hanging ledge as bait for investors. She often saw mine officials standing at the shaft collar, watching every bucket of ore that came from belowground and digging out some of the best specimens for themselves.

Stockholders grew restive when they saw no return on their investment. In an attempt to pacify them, the company sent out an engineer to appraise the situation at the mine. He returned a dismal report, saying that the operation lacked sufficient water, that the ore was low-grade, and that the machinery wasn't suitable for this kind of mining. Camp residents drifted back to Minnesota, taking souvenir pieces of the quartz ledge with them. The only real money realized by anyone connected to the Black Rock Company was the cash down payment to William and J.K.

Both Gen and J.K. felt that the mine could have returned a profit if it had been handled properly. J.K. wasn't ready to give up on the Black Rock District.

# THREE

## ∼ Saturday Night Celebrations

ANGIE STUDIED THE EVEN PROFILE and strong jawline of the young man driving the wagon and decided that despite a rapidly receding hairline he was quite handsome. Strong, sun-blackened hands handled the reins expertly, the kind of hands that could do anything, build anything. The driver, Joseph Hammer, reminded her of her own father.

This was in the summer of 1895, and Angie, now twenty-five, knew that the term "old maid schoolteacher" was being whispered behind her back. Her two youngest sisters had recently married — Addie to Charles Tweed, the son of the old territorial judge, and Monica to William Bell, a Phoenix physician. Still, Angie, quite happy with her life, wasn't in any hurry to find a husband. Friends and relatives kept telling her to quit waiting for the perfect man to come along.

Joseph Hammer's words interrupted her reverie. "Sometimes I think we should have stayed in El Paso. We had a thriving construction firm there with none of the union labor problems that we have here in Phoenix, but Mother wanted to move to Phoenix and live on a real farm, and Dad can't refuse her anything. He recently found this place out on Christie Road [now called McDowell Road] where Grand Avenue crosses the railroad tracks. Erna wants you to see the farm before she makes definite plans for her wedding. You know my sister. She can't make a move unless Angie approves."

Angie and Joseph's sister, Erna, had been close friends ever since the Hammers had moved next door to Angie's parents several years before. Angie liked this lively German family but now faced the loss of her only remaining single friend as Erna made plans to wed Richard Keyes, a businessman from El Paso. Erna had asked Joseph to ferry Angie out to the Hammer farm to help with wedding preparations, the first of many such trips they would make together. Love and marriage became a frequent topic of conversation.

Erna's gala wedding, staged in November of 1895, included a sumptuous banquet with music, dancing, and lots of German beer. William, normally a teetotaler, went overboard with his toasts to the bride and groom, while Sarah looked on disapprovingly. When William's consumption of beer didn't slacken, Sarah voiced concern to Angie. "Your papa is in no shape to drive home. If I know him, he'll try to make our horse climb a tree or some other silly stunt."

Joseph became the designated wagon driver that night.

### The Vows and the Aftermath

Some experts maintain that biological readiness and physical proximity have more to do with choosing a mate than love does. If so, this profile nicely fit Angie when she and Joseph exchanged vows six months later, on Easter Sunday of 1896.

Because Angie wrote in such detail about Erna's wedding in her memoirs, it's rather telling that she noted only the date of her own marriage and nothing else about the occasion. Undoubtedly, the ceremony took place during a solemn Catholic mass, and if a reception followed, it certainly didn't include German beer. One has to wonder what Sarah thought of her new son-in-law from a German Protestant family far removed from her own Irish Catholic heritage.

Rather telling, too, is the fact that the newlyweds stayed at the farm for many months until they found a place of their own. Angie probably helped fill the void that Erna's absence had left in the family circle, and she seemed to develop a closer bond with her mother- and father-in-law, Lena and Louis Hammer, than she did with her new husband.

Found among Angie's papers is the following brief story about Lena and Louis's bizarre experience as immigrants to America, written as Lena told it to Angie. This is why Joseph said, "My dad can't refuse anything my mother wants."

Angela and Joseph Hammer pose for a wedding portrait in 1896.
(Original photograph by the Elite Studio in Phoenix)

Louis and I both emigrated from Germany as teenagers. After my mother died, my father remarried, and I couldn't remain in the same household with my stepmother, so my father let my brother and me come to the United States.

I was working in Chicago as a maid when I met Louis Schlegel. We married when we were both nineteen. He had a good job in construction, so by the time we had four children, Louis was well established as a building contractor.

Louis's associates persuaded him to change his name to something that sounded more American. In German, Schlegel means a flail or hammer-like weapon of war, so Louis chose Hammer to be our new last name.

One day it was terribly hot and humid. Thinking it might rain, Louis went to cover some cement in the basement of a building under construction. He was overcome by the heat and lay unconscious in that sweltering basement for hours before someone found him. He couldn't go back to work and lost his job with the construction firm. The doctors said he might never fully recover from the heat stroke.

When Louis could get around a little better, my brother took him to El Paso to help him get established in construction work there. Then my brother returned to Chicago.

At first, Louis sent money and letters, but after a year or so, I didn't hear from him any more. My brother told me that Louis had probably died, and he gave me money to help support my children.

After a few years, I remarried, and we moved to a farm. By the time my second husband died, my sons were old enough to take over the farm work. I liked the farm life, but as my sons grew older they didn't want to remain there.

Then another man wanted to marry me, and I gave my consent. A few days before my wedding, a friend rushed into my home saying, "Lena, Lena, Louis still lives!"

At first, I couldn't believe it, but my friend said she had actually talked to Louis and found out that he had been sneaking into town to check on us from time to time. He wanted to see me but didn't want to interfere with my plans to marry. I asked my friend to bring Louis to me. I wouldn't marry again as long as he lived.

We were very angry with each other at first. He wanted to know why I hadn't answered his letters. "What letters?" I asked. "You quit writing and sending money. If it hadn't been for my brother, we would have starved to death."

Eventually, we realized that it was my brother who had been keeping us apart

**all those years. He'd done a wicked thing by telling me Louis was dead, with-holding his letters, and making me think the money Louis sent was from him. He thought he was doing me a favor by keeping us apart because he didn't want me to remain with a man whose wits had been addled by a heat stroke.**

**When Louis and I reunited, we lived in El Paso for awhile, then brought our children to Phoenix with us to start a new life here.**

Angie was expecting by the time she and Joe moved from the farm into one of the three houses that Gen and J.K. owned on Third Avenue. It was a rather communal arrangement, with the couples eating together and Gen's little toddler, Veva, running in and out of both homes with abandon. Joe and J.K. became inseparable. These were happy times for Angie.

Joe continued working in his father's construction company. Angie observed what impact that situation had on the family:

**When the firm was awarded a contract, there was a celebration. When the job was finished, there was a celebration, and every Saturday night, there was a celebration.**

It's uncertain what Angie meant when she used the term "celebration." Certainly, she knew the celebrations involved the use of alcohol. At first, she didn't seem to mind, but her attitude changed when Joe and J.K. came home from the tavern late one night.

Joe was so incoherent that at first Angie thought he was sick. When she finally understood the real nature of his condition, she couldn't believe the drastic change in his personality. She told him he wasn't the same man she thought she had married. This comment so enraged Joe that he swore at her and stomped out of the house without his hat.

Little Veva, hiding in another room, came creeping out with Joe's hat. She told Angie not to worry, that she was here to protect her aunt. Angie wrote,

**It finally dawned on me that the child had been through frightening times with her own father and knew an intoxicated man when she saw one. I was almost persuaded to quit the marriage at once, but a baby was on the way. I convinced myself he probably wouldn't do it again.**

Joe and J.K. began spending more and more time at the tavern. J.K., an aspiring politician, adhered to the policy of discussing politics over mugs of beer. Joe went along for support and to drown his own woes about the local building unions eating into the profits of his father's construction firm. Angie and Gen agreed that they had a problem on their hands.

With these black clouds of discontent hovering over both households, Angie told Gen that this baby would be her last. She would never bring another child into a marriage with such a shaky foundation. "I guess if it's a boy, I'll have to give him enough names to honor both sides of the family. What do you think of Louis Joseph Fairfax Hammer? That will take care of Joe, his father, and a Fairfax relative on my father's side. I've always liked the name Fairfax. It sounds so distinguished."

Grandpa Louis's namesake arrived in April of 1897, but the baby would be called "Louie" to forestall confusion over their names. While Joe and J.K. passed out cigars at the tavern, Grandmother Sarah proclaimed the baby was destined to become a priest. "See how he makes the sign of the cross with his little hands!"

J.K. and Gen's marriage continued to deteriorate. When Gen said she was ready to call it quits, Angie suggested that the two couples sit down together to have a serious talk about the situation.

The boys readily agreed that their close living arrangement made it easy to be a bad influence on each other. After much discussion, all parties agreed, for the sake of their marriages, that they should live apart. J.K. still retained an interest in the mine at Black Rock. He and his family would go there to live while he did some mining and dried out. Joe and Angie came up with a more radical solution. They would leave Phoenix entirely, move to Los Angeles, and start over from scratch. Since heavy drinking seemed to be the hallmark of the construction trades, they would look for a different kind of enterprise. No sacrifice was too great now that they had one child and another on the way.

Despite Angie's intentions, she had found herself again in the family way. Although this pregnancy would be a hardship, Angie and Joe both believed that learning to depend more on each other and less on family would strengthen their marriage.

The news of this upcoming move broke Grandpa Louis's heart. He would be losing not only his cherished grandson but also his son, who had played such a vital role in his business. So, not long after Angie and Joe left town, Lena agreed to leave the farm and Louis sold his construction firm. They moved back to El Paso to be with Erna and her children. Without Joe and Angie, they had no reason to remain in Phoenix.

Angie and Joe scouted around Los Angeles for a few days, trying to get oriented. They probably had a small nest egg, and they looked for an income-producing investment property in this rapidly growing city. After finding a newspaper ad for a property on Temple Street, they went to investigate. It was a two-story building with a small delicatessen on the ground floor and rental apartments on the second floor. Angie described the place:

> **The delicatessen looked ever so nice with its clean-looking stock of cereals and packaged goods. We sat around awhile and watched a number of customers come in for lunch or for carryout food. Even though we weren't even average business people and knew very little about cooking, we took over the lease and went to work with great hopes of future prosperity.**

The two innocents from Arizona soon found they'd been easy marks for Los Angeles con artists. Ninety percent of the packages on the deli shelves were empty. Since they didn't know where to find the crooks who had fleeced them, they renewed the stock and went to work cooking breakfasts and lunches.

But being fleeced wasn't the worst part; they soon discovered that they had bought a tenement house full of rats. At night, they would lie in bed and listen to the sound of rats scurrying inside the plaster walls of the building. They read newspaper articles about rats invading office buildings and chewing up checks and records. The entire city was under siege.

One night Angie crept downstairs in an effort to determine the extent of the rat problem in their deli. She sat on the stove, blew out her candle, and waited to see if a rat would appear. In a few minutes, hordes of rats swarmed all over the kitchen. She screamed for Joe, and they set about trying to determine how the rodents had gained entrance to the kitchen. Each time they patched one entry hole, the rats gnawed their way through another hole. In desperation, they put the building up for sale.

While they awaited a buyer for the property and during the last stage of Angie's pregnancy, Monica came to help out in the deli. Baby William, named for Angie's father, arrived in May of 1899.

After the property sold, probably at a great loss, Joe had no choice but to return to construction. This began a series of moves from one rat-, flea-, or bedbug-infested rental property to another, as Angie tried to follow Joe to construction sites in different areas around Los Angeles. The better rentals refused children, and often Joe had to travel great distances from home to work or else remain at the job site during the week. Without the support of husband or family, Angie became a transient in a big city, trying to cope with the pressures of motherhood. One episode illustrates her desperation during this time.

Angie hadn't noticed the railroad tracks hidden behind some backyard shrubbery in one rental. She saw only the fenced-in yard with a nice sandpile for little Louie. Because of the home's location, Joe would have to be gone during the workweek, a disadvantage, to be sure but a price that would have to be paid for the perfect home.

Louie developed an inordinate fear of the trains that came roaring down the tracks, shaking the foundation of the house, but Angie told herself the child would eventually get used to it. Each morning when she put the baby down for a nap, she sent Louie out to the sandpile to play with his blocks and toys, hoping to catch a little shut-eye herself. Invariably, just as the baby got to sleep, an oncoming train would send Louie shrieking into the house and she would have two hysterical youngsters to calm. Angie would jounce the pair of them on the bed and, in her words, "perform all kinds of idiocies" while she was in a state of near-collapse herself.

The climax of her endurance came the day that Billy had a fever. She tried to give the baby a dose of castor oil mixed with orange juice, but he refused to drink out of the thick-rimmed coffee cup and either pursed his lips tightly or spat it all over her. She described her breaking point:

**After five trials of new doses, I went to pieces and hurled that horrid coffee cup toward the baby. It came within a hair's breadth of striking him on the head, but something deflected my aim, and the cup struck the wall with an awful thud.**

Terribly frightened by what she had almost done, Angie gathered up her babies, and all three cried themselves out of tears.

After the crying episode, Angie's pragmatic self surfaced to take charge of the situation. First of all, she needed to do something to allay Louie's fear of trains. She took the youngster and his toy train out to the sandpile and remained with him. The minute she saw the train coming, she realized his problem. From that angle, it looked as if the train were bearing right down on top of the sandpile. She picked up the toy train and said, "Let's compare your baby choo-choo to the big papa choo-choo. Your baby doesn't have steam around its wheels, but otherwise, they are just alike. See the engine, the whistle, and the caboose."

Louie smiled through his tears as he compared the trains. From then on, he became an aficionado of trains. This helped restore some of Angie's faith in herself as a mother, but it didn't help her problem of sleep deprivation.

In less than two years, Angie, again pregnant, pleaded with Joe to return to Arizona. She had a cough that wouldn't go away and felt so poorly that she doubted she could make it through another pregnancy alone. In one sense, they had achieved their original objective because they had indeed learned to depend on each other—whenever Joe was around.

Then a letter arrived from Grandpa Louis asking Joe to come to El Paso to work with his new Caples and Hammer Construction Company. They thought maybe this would work out even better than returning to family in Phoenix. Joe left for El Paso at once, while Angie stayed behind to take care of moving arrangements.

## That Dreaded Gray Fungus

Angie bragged that Louie and Billy were great travelers on the trip to El Paso.

**The children gave me very little trouble, and train passengers nearly always played with them. Billy was so pretty, with his large blue eyes and golden curls, that I tried to make a girl of him. I had him togged in a white lace and embroidery dress, white stockings and slippers, and a lace bonnet. He was the most beautiful child in the waiting room at El Paso.**

When Grandpa Louis met them at the train station, Angie's pseudo-girl slid off the bench and ran across the room on sturdy boy legs. A thoroughly masculine laugh came from under the child's dainty bonnet. Grandpa Louis and Joe didn't take kindly to Billy's dress and sent Angie and Erna shopping for Buster Brown outfits the next day.

Angie, however, continued to make the child wear bonnets to protect his beautiful skin until the men's teasing became unbearable. Angie quit entering Billy in baby beauty contests and awaited her next baby, hoping that it would be a girl.

Angie settled into a new house on Myrtle Street across from Erna and close to her beloved in-laws. She busied herself with "nesting in" chores, planting grass and flowers and making clothes for the coming baby, but this period of domestic tranquility wasn't to last.

Lena's sudden death sent the whole Hammer clan into a spin. While Angie and Louis grieved over Lena, Louis and Lena's four children went after their mother's share of the parents' estate. This display of avarice sent Louis to a real estate attorney, but he eventually distributed his property and assets to his children to quell their bickering. Angie was appalled.

St. Patrick's Day in 1902 brought Angie and Joe another baby boy. She put aside any longing for a girl child after one look at the new arrival's cherubic face, but she had run out of male family names. Wanting to cheer up Grandpa Louis, she gave him the honor of naming the baby. He chose Marvin, the name of an attorney whom he greatly admired.

An accepted aspect of motherhood in early days was the nursing of young children through rounds of communicable disease. Erna's and Angie's children played together, swapping measles, mumps, and chicken pox, so Angie wasn't alarmed when both Louie and Billy began running a fever. But when she discovered gray patches of fungus in their noses and throats, she knew what it meant: diphtheria! Only a few years before, those patches would have signaled a death sentence, but a therapeutic serum had recently been developed.

When the doctor was summoned to give the boys a shot of the antitoxin, Angie asked him whether her five-month-old infant might contract the disease. He assured her that a breast-fed newborn would have natural immunity.

Before long, though, baby Marvin began coughing and seemed to have difficulty catching his breath. His throat was clear, but there, in one of the baby's nostrils, was the dreaded grayish white fungus! In a panic, she called the doctor back to their house.

The doctor avoided Angie's eyes as he checked the baby. "It's very unusual, but, yes, the baby does have diphtheria."

"Will you give him the shot?" Angie asked.

"He's too young for the antitoxin. Mrs. Hammer, I know this is hard, but you must prepare for the worst. Be thankful that you already have two fine, healthy boys." So saying, the doctor snapped shut his bag with an air of finality and hurried out the front door.

Angie went into shock, unable to speak or even think. Staring vacantly into space, she rocked the baby, humming softly. Hours passed. Peeking in on her occasionally, Joe and Erna thought she had gone off the deep end.

Suddenly she jumped to her feet, put the baby in his crib, and set a jar of carbolated Vaseline into a pan of water on the stove. When the Vaseline had liquefied, she put the baby on her lap, filled an eyedropper with the liquid, and drop by drop slowly squeezed the contents into the baby's nostrils. Marvin sputtered and choked until he threw up the Vaseline. By the end of twenty-four hours, the gray fungus had disappeared and Marvin was sleeping peacefully.

At this stage of Angie's life, the progression of unfortunate events seemed endless. No sooner were the children restored to health than a letter came from her mother in Wickenburg. Papa William was seriously ill with cirrhosis of the liver. Angie should come at once if she hoped to see him alive.

Hastily, Angie left her two older sons in Erna's care. She and baby Marvin took the next train to Arizona.

Finding her father in considerable pain, she couldn't help smiling as he complained about the medicine he had to take for his terrible gas pains. "It's worse than nine kinds of cat dung, and believe me, I've been given all nine kinds."

As it turned out, baby Marvin proved to be William's best medicine. William kept his newest grandchild on the bed with him day and night, and Angie watched both their dispositions brighten as the child tugged at his beard and romped all over him.

Old Henry Wickenburg, clad in standard red flannel shirt and overalls, came to see William every day. Along with lots of advice, he brought tea leaves made from rabbitbrush, which was said to be a blood purifier. Henry called it "whorehouse tea."

During these daily visits, Henry would occasionally talk about himself. Angie paid close attention to these conversations because there were already many rumors about the man.

**I heard Henry say that he was related to the Krupps, famous munitions manufacturers in Essen, Germany. As a young man, he had been reported to the police for digging coal under his own home without permission from the authorities. Fearing arrest, he came to America to escape the tyranny of his own**

**country and adopted the surname of his maternal grandmother, whose maiden name was Wickenburg. His own name was Heinrich Heinsel.**

She also heard Henry talk about his "Indian spirit guide," who left letters under his pillow at night. Some of these letters came from his mother and extolled the beauty of "the other side." She urged him to come, too. Henry told about one letter he'd received recently that left instructions for handling his financial affairs. It advised him to deed all his property to his caretaker, Helene Holland. Henry asked Sarah, "What d'you think, Mrs. Hutch? I can't understand why my mother, who couldn't speak anything but German when she lived, now writes letters in English. Goddam if I know what to make of it."

Sarah replied, "What I think, Henry, is that someone is making a fool of you. You know very well that, if your mother could communicate with you, she would write in German. I think someone is after your property, and you had better find out if you have living relatives in Germany before you make out your will."

Henry protested. "No, no, my Indian guide says that I haven't a relative left in this world. If you don't believe I'm the last of my tribe, Mrs. Hutch, you can write back home to Germany. I will not care."

Angie said her mother actually did take it upon herself to write the parish priest in Essen to ask if Henry's relatives still lived there. Further, she explained in her letter that Henry's caretakers would inherit considerable property if none of his German relatives came forward. Why she went to this trouble is anyone's guess. Was she meddling, or did she suspect Henry's caretakers of writing the fraudulent letters?

The priest wrote back to say that he had talked with Henry's relatives, and none were interested in giving up their German citizenship to claim Henry's property in the United States.

By the end of January, Joe had sent word that Angie should come home; the children needed their mother. Reluctantly, Angie left her father's bedside.

**I realized that my father was near the end of his life's journey, but he was so bright and kind even in his pain.**

**I could not return for the funeral in Wickenburg on February 22, 1903 but was thankful for the precious time I did get to spend with him.**

### For the Good of the Order

Not long after Angie returned to El Paso, a tiny, frail old lady appeared on her doorstep and introduced herself as Aunt Loyola, one of Sarah's sisters. Angie had a vague recollection of her mother describing such an aunt living in Mexico, so she welcomed the little old lady into her home. Loyola readily immersed herself in family life, helping with the children and other chores. She spoke English with a pronounced Mexican accent.

Little by little Angie put together the story of Aunt Loyola's life. In the early 1850s, Loyola had been encouraged by her own mother to enter a cloistered nunnery at the age of sixteen. Loyola lived there for some years, then left the nunnery for reasons known only to herself. A nun could not return to her convent if she remained away from her order for more than twenty-four hours. If that happened, she either had to return to her biological family or establish an order of her own. Loyola went to Mazatlán in Mexico, began a school there, and remained for many years. When the Mexican government had recently driven all Catholic institutions out of the country, this courageous lady had been left penniless and homeless. How she had found her way to Angie's doorstep remained a mystery.

What Loyola wanted more than anything in the world was to return to some Catholic order and live out her life in prayer and contemplation. Angela promised to help her as much as she could, but in the meantime Aunt Loyola would be welcome to remain in the Hammer household.

Angie hadn't felt well since she returned from Wickenburg, and she attributed her run-down condition to depression over the death of her father. Terrible coughing spells occasionally brought up blood. When Erna noticed that Angie's arms were a sickly green color, Joe blamed it on El Paso's cold, windy weather and insisted that Angie return to Wickenburg's dry climate and sunshine until her health improved. Secretly, Joe and Lena suspected Angie had tuberculosis.

Soon Angie, her three children, and Aunt Loyola boarded a train bound for Wickenburg. Angie's temperature spiraled during the trip. Passengers, alarmed at her coughing, gave her plenty of room. When a kindly doctor on the train came to her aid, he told her, "You aren't a 'lunger.' You just have a bad case of pneumonia."

In Wickenburg Angie got a rather chilly reception from her mother. Not only was Sarah shocked at Angie's frail appearance, she feared she would be forced into taking care of Loyola. Angie observed,

**I was blamed for bringing Loyola back with me. Mother had hoped that the old lady had found refuge in another convent by this time, but that was easier said than done.**

    **Loyola wouldn't eat at a table in the presence of men, and she was almost frightened by modern inventions such as electric lights, automobiles, and streetcars. Never before had she seen store windows filled with merchandise. Mother considered her helpless, and they could not get along.**

Angie began writing to priests and bishops throughout the West about Loyola's predicament. Finally a convent in California consented to take her. Angie had the satisfaction of knowing that Aunt Loyola would end her days happily after a lifetime of service to others.

### A Few Terse Comments

Angie soon found another reason she had been feeling so poorly. In addition to the pneumonia, she was pregnant. Without elaborating on any details, she further explained that she fell, had a miscarriage, and began to hemorrhage.

Joe came from El Paso to be with her. They rented a house in Phoenix, and Angie placed herself under the care of her brother-in-law, Dr. William Bell. Dr. Bell performed some sort of emergency surgery, possibly a hysterectomy, that Angie said saved her life.

The story of Angie's seven-year marriage ends with these terse comments: "Joe acts up and drinks. I apply for divorce. It's granted in 1903, and I move to Wickenburg."

Angie left us with little information about Joseph Hammer as a person or the culminating months of their marriage. Memories can be painful, as her final notation on the marriage indicates:

**The period from 1897 to 1903 contains nothing of historical value or even a memory to be treasured, due to the absence of some steadying influence such as Alcoholics Anonymous. It became necessary for me in 1903 to seek a di-**

**vorce, mainly, I felt, in the interests of my children, who lost a potentially good
father to alcohol.**

It is doubtful that Angie ever obtained a legal divorce from Joseph Hammer.
At that time, a divorce would have required an act of the territorial legislature
and officials of the Catholic Church.

# FOUR

## ⌒ A Pig in a Poke

VERY LITTLE REMAINS SECRET in a town of only three hundred people, and gossip about Angie's divorce and her experience as a typesetter at the *Phoenix Gazette* had not escaped the ears of one Mrs. Harriet Wilson. Ostensibly on a social call to express her concern about Angela's health, Mrs. Wilson paid a visit to Sarah's home in Wickenburg, where Angie was recuperating from her surgery and her divorce.

Mrs. Wilson came straight out and asked how Angie intended to support her children. Angie confessed that this concern had caused her many a sleepless night. She couldn't return to the long hours of schoolteaching with three youngsters in tow, and she'd heard nothing from Joe after he'd left her a five-hundred-dollar note and returned to El Paso.

Mrs. Wilson had a solution. "Out of the goodness of my heart, I will sell you my newspaper, the *Wickenburg Miner*, lock, stock, and barrel, for a trifling 250 dollars. With your background in newspaper work and your fine education, I know you can make a go of it. I wouldn't think of making this offer to another living soul because it's worth a whole lot more. My paper enjoys advertising from almost all the business establishments in this town, even some in Prescott. I've brought my subscription list for you to look over."

As Angie looked over the impressive list of subscribers, a loud squeaking noise came from outside the kitchen door. The two women rushed outside to see little Marvin busily pumping water from a well in the backyard. Mrs. Wilson exclaimed, "Can you beat that? A two-year-old child who already knows how to pump water! I must write an article about him for the paper."

Captivated by seeing her son's name in print in the next issue of the *Miner*,

Angie didn't hesitate to give Mrs. Wilson a hundred dollars as down payment for the paper and a note for the remaining 150 dollars. She couldn't imagine a more rewarding livelihood than owning a newspaper. She would be able to write, conduct her newspaper business, and take care of her boys all at the same time. For her, things always seemed so simple in the beginning.

### Five Gallons of Crude Vaseline

Taking inventory of her purchase, Angie found a Washington handpress, one of those old toggle-and-lever flatbed letterpresses from the 1830s that weigh over a ton. Mrs. Wilson had seldom used this press because her papers were printed in Phoenix and shipped to Wickenburg. She used the Washington only when she needed to comply with a government ruling that land notices had to be printed locally. A little ink, a brayer for spreading the ink on the type, and a mailing table completed the inventory. Oh, yes, there was one more curious item — a five-gallon can of crude Vaseline. As an occupational sideline, Mrs. Wilson produced and sold some sort of cure-all ointment.

Angie set about contacting the merchants on Mrs. Wilson's list of advertisers. One after another, they sadly shook their heads. No, they had not authorized any ads that may have appeared in the *Miner*; they only advertised in the *News-Herald*. They supposed Mrs. Wilson had used their ads as complimentary fillers to give the appearance of a prosperous newspaper.

Disappointed about the advertising but still hopeful, Angie contacted some of the people whose names appeared on Mrs. Wilson's subscription list. When she learned that those names represented only people who had been contacted about buying stock in Unida Mining and Milling, her heart sank even further. Mrs. Wilson and her partner, Mr. Nickerson, were the principal stockholders in Unida, a copper company they were promoting. The *Miner* was nothing more than a free advertising sheet for Unida. Angie had bought a pig in a poke!

Eli Perkins owned the town's real newspaper, the *News-Herald*, whose history went back to the Hall Brothers and J. O. Dunbar. In 1901 Dick and Ernest Hall, ousted from the territorial secretary's office by another appointee, cast about for a new occupation and realized that Wickenburg didn't have a newspaper. Dick began rounding up news in Wickenburg and sending it to Ernest in Phoenix to be printed by the *Republican*. Meanwhile, J. O. Dunbar of the

*Phoenix Evening Gazette*, a rival of the *Republican*, came out with the *Wickenburg Herald* the same week that the Halls' *Wickenburg Times* made its debut. Soon after this, the two papers consolidated as the *Wickenburg News-Herald* when Dunbar sold his paper to the Hall brothers.

Old Henry Wickenburg, pleased that the town had a newspaper of its own, donated a lot on Tegner Street to the Halls for a newspaper office. As a show of gratitude, Dick adopted the first part of Wickenburg's last name as his middle name. From then on, he called himself Dick Wick Hall.

The intrepid Dick Wick, on his way to becoming an expert in mining and land promoting, as well as Arizona's leading humorist, couldn't remain in a stuffy newspaper office for long. He sold the *News-Herald* to Eli Perkins in 1903 and took off to tramp the hills with his gold pan.

By the time Angie bought the *Miner* in 1905, Eli had moved the *News-Herald* away from Wickenburg in Maricopa County to Martinez, sixteen miles away in Yavapai County. In those days anyone could establish a town site for a mere 160 dollars, and the mine at nearby Congress looked very promising. Speculating on a grand outcome for the mine and the hundreds of people who would soon clamor for land, Eli bought the town site and moved his printing equipment there. Although Wickenburg's merchants were a little miffed that the paper had been moved out of town, they continued to support the *News-Herald*.

Wickenburg residents didn't know what to make of the impoverished so-called divorcée who seemed determined to give their town another newspaper. Few thought she could last over the long haul in a field dominated exclusively by men, but some fell under her charms. Though at first hesitant to subscribe to the *Miner*, townspeople soon exchanged produce from their gardens and orchards for advertising or newspaper subscriptions. They liked her chatty little tabloid and knew she had no mining or land agenda of her own to promote. However, mining was the Wickenburg area's stock in trade, and Angie had to sharpen her reporting skills on the subject.

> **Since I didn't know enough about the mining industry to risk my own version of technical matters, I interviewed every well-known mining man or engineer who visited Wickenburg. From the Lewishon Brothers, who were copper mining men, to Walter Harvey Reed, I gleaned enough knowledge to keep on the straight and narrow path in my reporting of mining news.**

In some of her articles, Angie panned the greenhorn superintendents that eastern companies sent to oversee local mining operations, men who had no understanding of hard-rock mining, much less the culture of their Mexican workers. She often quoted Mark Twain's famous line, "A gold mine is a hole in the ground with a liar at the top." Some of her articles began appearing in mining journals around the country.

Editors at the time were expected to "boom" the virtues of their particular locality. As Angie extolled the virtues of Wickenburg's mild climate, its lush produce grown along the river, and the good works of its citizens, people began seeing their town in a new way—through the eyes of their spirited editor. Subscriptions trickled in. After securing her first half-page ad, Angie felt that the *Miner* had at last emerged as a viable newspaper. The editor out at Martinez watched these developments with apprehension.

Her first headline story came about on one quiet afternoon in 1905 as her sons attended a baseball game. Using this respite to catch up on some writing at the office, she heard someone calling her name.

### Spirits Call Henry

William Holland, the husband of Henry Wickenburg's caretaker, Helene Holland, didn't bother to use the gate. He climbed over a wire fence, red-faced and out of breath. "Come quick, Mrs. Hammer! Henry just shot himself! He's down in the grove! Go stay with him until I can find a lawman."

Angie hurried to the grove and found Henry Wickenburg lying on his side, his knees somewhat flexed, and a pistol on the ground nearby. In no time, others rushed to the spot. Soon the ground around Henry was so trampled that any footprints or evidence left behind by the victim or a possible murder suspect had been wiped out. William Holland returned with J. K. Murphy. J.K. impaneled a coroner's jury on the spot, and since there was no evidence of foul play, the jury had no choice but to declare Henry's death a suicide.

Many around Wickenburg refused to believe that Henry Wickenburg would take his own life. He had seemed quite content, and Angie described him as a friendly, garrulous man who welcomed old-timers into his tiny hut to swap stories. Those who knew him as well as Angie's mother also knew that the Hollands were to be the recipients of his estate and that Henry had attached a codicil to his will giving himself the right to dispose of his own property as long as he lived. Of late, he had been selling plenty of his lots for ten dollars apiece. Who had written those suspicious letters from his Indian spirit guide? Had the spirits who had been calling him for so long become tired of waiting?

Surrounded by chairs for the mourners, Henry's casket rested under a very large mesquite tree on a knoll in front of his cabin. Mrs. Holland's pet parrot lived in this same tree, and now the parrot sat on a low branch, quietly taking note of the gathering crowd. A woman wearing a large black bow on top of her head and dressed in a rather short skirt came tripping up the path like a sixteen-year-old. When Polly saw the woman, she squawked, "Good Lord, God Amighty! Don't she think she's dressed up!"

Spasms of laughter engulfed the crowd as Mrs. Holland reprimanded Polly and tried to get her into the house. Polly sought higher branches and then cocked her head and inquired dolefully, "What's-a matta? Too bad, Polly, too bad!"

After quiet and dignity had been restored, the minister prayed for the soul of the departed pioneer. Angie noted,

**He extolled Henry's virtues, while minimizing the seven lone graves on Boot Hill, occupied by the unfortunates who had tried to steal the goods and chattels of the deceased. [Probably well-known hearsay at the time.]**

After the funeral service, hundreds of people waited for over an hour to hear the reading of the will. No one was surprised that Henry had conveyed his property to the Hollands. People began mumbling under their breath. One said, "I don't blame her for shooting the old man."

Another answered, "She realized that Heaven is a much more comfortable place than this cruel earth."

Other wisecrackers chimed in. "Who knows but what that old body has been sidetracked by the spirit of youth within? Maybe he'll grow new whiskers without a single gray hair in the lot."

Angie added her own musings to this gossip.

**Having read and heard so many of Ripley's *Believe It or Not* stories that prove people innocent in the face of the most damning evidence, I chose to give the Hollands the benefit of the doubt. Helene had been really good to Henry. Never**

**before had he been fed and kept as clean as he was during the last few years of his life.**

**Henry Cowell, a pioneer merchant who kept records of every death in Wickenburg, wrote "Henry Wickenburg *killed*, 1905."**

## Hobos and Prophetic Dreams

About the time the *Miner* began edging toward the black, Eli Perkins came in from Congress with a proposition for Angie. The *Miner* had taken a sizable chunk out of his *News-Herald* readership. "Mrs. Hammer, don't you think Wickenburg has one too many newspapers for such a small neighborhood? Why don't we consolidate so we can both make a living? We could combine our legal notices and you could continue on as the *Miner*'s representative and correspondent, running it just as you're doing now. I'll do all the printing at my Congress plant and support your policy of promoting Wickenburg interests."

Angie was delighted. No longer would she need to crank out over twelve hundred sheets of newsprint each week. Eli would have all the financial headaches, and she would have more time to devote to the children and to writing news of the town, the part of newspaper work that she really loved.

However, it came as a shock one day when Eli approached her. "Angie, where's your editorial matter?"

She shrieked in alarm. "Editorial matter? I couldn't write an editorial to save my life!"

"Angie, you've been writing editorials all along, but we've been calling them articles. You remind me of the story you told about your son who wouldn't eat a muffin, but if you called it a popover, he'd gobble it up. It must be the same characteristic breaking out in both of you."

Eli didn't mention the word "editorial" again or even compliment her on her writing for fear of freezing her up. Instead he said, "Time to get your copy in so I can edit your split infinitives and mixed-up verbs."

Eli's paper carried a tantalizing slogan above its masthead—"Get Next to the Gold." He and Angie wrote continuously about discoveries at Congress, Octave, Grijalva, and Oro Grande. When Dick Wick came in from his prospecting trips, he paraded fine specimens of "picture gold" in front of Eli.

After a few blissful months, Angie's new working arrangement took an abrupt turn. Eli became a victim of his own glowing reports of the gold that awaited any inveterate prospector. "If you'll buy me out for five thousand, I'll make the terms easy. I'll even stay long enough to show you how to use the printing equipment."

Angie was dumbfounded. "Are you serious? You know I don't have that kind of money, just a little mining stock."

"I'll take whatever you have in trade, and you can give me a note for the rest."

Over the next few days, Eli and Angie reached a settlement. Angie owned several lots in Wickenburg that she had traded for a lot in the Brill Addition in Phoenix. She also owned a block of stock in the Consolidated Union Grand Mining Company, a promising copper property. Eli took the lots and the stock as a down payment, and they agreed to split all the forthcoming money from a printing contract the paper held with Yavapai County. Angie signed a note for the rest of the five thousand dollars.

Along with the *News-Herald* and the *Miner*, Angie now owned the title to an adobe building that housed Eli's printing equipment at Congress. This equipment included a Country Campbell cylinder press that she didn't know how to operate, some job printing machinery for commercial work, and some supplies. Most of all, this purchase included doubts about her ability to handle the whole operation.

Eli remained until it appeared that Angie knew what she was doing with the machinery. Before leaving, he told her, "Angie, now you get to write all the editorials by yourself."

Angie waved him off with a smile. "I thought we were never going to mention the word 'editorial' again."

Angie and the boys moved to Congress and took up residence in a building situated just west of the Santa Fe, Prescott and Phoenix Railroad. She immediately began a series of profiles about Congress's forty to fifty residents. She wrote about the Williams' dairy, the Johnsons, who ran the section house, and Rufus Cannon, who, even with a crippled leg, could mount a horse and throw a steer faster than his brother Lucius with two good legs. And to her later dismay, she wrote about Richard and John Bullard, who owned the general merchandise store and saloon east of the tracks.

**Richard Bullard was such a stickler for words that he became quite indignant if someone said, "Is that so?" He took this response to mean that his word was being doubted.**

Richard had promised Angie a new dress if she would write business letters for him. He told her she could have any kind of dress she wanted, but first he had to sell his mine. She knew this would never happen, but she wrote his letters anyway. He'd had many opportunities to sell, but no one could meet his terms — a hundred thousand dollars in cold, hard cash.

In her write-up about the Bullard brothers, Angie described John's saloon patrons as "a welkin ring of night hawks." John took serious offense at this description, perhaps not realizing that "welkin" only referred to the sky. He sent word to Angie that her printing plant would be reduced to rubble if she ever wrote about him or his patrons again. Although unnerved, she didn't make an issue of the threat.

Hobo printers became the bane of Angie's existence at Congress. As word spread along the rails that Angie would never refuse these itinerant printers at least a few hours of work, they flocked to the *Miner*. To repay her kindness, they generally did more work than required before joining John Bullard's "welkin ring of night hawks." However, Angie could never depend on them.

It may have been the worry about printers or it may have been sleeping outside close to the noise of the railroad that caused Angie to begin having rather unusual and prophetic dreams. One dream was about a printer whose home was on fire. Although she tried to help him by beating down the flames with her hands, the printer suffered serious injuries.

The next morning this printer didn't show up for work. Since she had an overflow of job printing on hand, she went to his house and found him still in bed. Before she could take him to task for his laziness, he pointed to the charred wall behind his cookstove with red, blistered hands. Coals from his stove had fallen into the wood box and started a fire in the night.

Had her dream been prophetic? She must have shuddered at the thought and she resolved that if such a dream were to occur again, she would wake up and go investigate.

A few nights later, she awoke from a dream that Eli Perkins' little boy had fallen into a deep pond in the Hassayampa River and was drowning. The dream was so vivid that she got up to call Eli to make sure the child was all right. Just then her phone rang. It was Eli calling to tell her that his son had almost drowned in the river.

You can be sure that Angie paid more attention to her dreams from then on, but none was as prophetic as these two. She did report one more dream that left a big impression on her, and maybe it was prophetic in a way.

In this dream, she had a secret hideout in a mountain cleft above Congress. She had no trouble getting there, but there was an easy way and a hard way to get out. The hard way involved winding around the cliff until she emerged on top and then carefully picking her way down to avoid falling into cracks. The easy way meant going through a certain cave that emerged at ground level. However, in this cave, a Damocleslike sword could fall at any moment. When she discovered that there really was a cave in the mountain with a precariously balanced rock that could fall without warning, she wondered if this dream implied that she should be more careful about the choices she was making.

## Wickenburg Wants Its Newspaper

When Angie and her former partner, Eli Perkins, discovered that the title to the building that housed the printing plant was defective, he credited her note with five hundred dollars. They continued to split the proceeds from their Yavapai County printing contract until she paid off his entire note in 1907.

Eli didn't come out as well on the stock from Consolidated Union that he had agreed to take from Angie as the down payment on the printing plant. Dividends from this stock financed his gold prospecting until, without warning, the price of copper dropped from thirty-seven cents a pound to nine cents. Eli had to go back to work. In Prescott, he connected with that town's newspaper, also called the *Miner*, and continued to stay in close contact with Angie.

When Wickenburg businessmen learned that Angie needed new quarters for the printing plant, they clamored for her to move the *Miner* back to town. Except for the huge expense of moving heavy printing machinery into Wickenburg, Angie had no reason to remain in Congress. They took up a collection to help with this moving cost. Angie wrote,

> **Getting all that machinery carted back to Wickenburg was a terrible job, but I was glad to get back to the old town. First, we moved into a large store building, on the lower floor of what would become the Charlesbois Hotel and later, into the Root Building, where the *Miner* remained until 1912.**

Printers labored under terrible lighting conditions in early print shops, nearsightedly squinting at small type under the dim light of kerosene lamps.

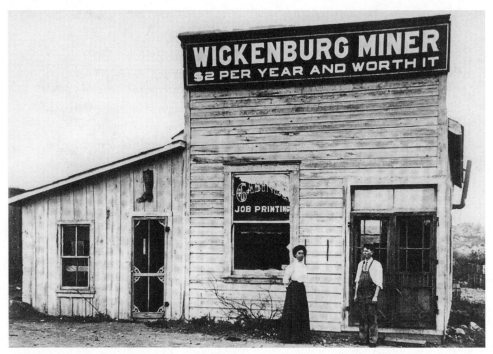

Angie and printer Tom Kellis stand in front of the *Miner* building. S. R. Hill painted the sign. The word "Cabinet" etched into the window is a remnant of the building's former days as the Cabinet Saloon.

Angela in the office of the *Wickenburg Miner*. Note the telephone on the wall. Telephone service came to Wickenburg in 1902.

Angie attempted to correct this problem by installing carbide acetylene lighting in the *Miner* plant. These lights were fed by flammable gas from an acetylene generator and consisted of two galvanized iron vats—a smaller tank turned bottom side up inside another tank fixed so that water would drip on the carbide to make gas. Heavy weights on the gas tank created enough pressure to keep the vat from blowing up. Although this setup provided better lighting, the weights rumbled alarmingly at times, increasing the danger of fire. That, combined with the use of flammable liquids to clean ink from used type, caused Angie to live with the specter of fire on a daily basis.

However, the fire that almost destroyed the *Miner* building didn't come from within the plant. It began in a home between the post office and the *Miner*'s quarters, the Collins house. Just as with the printer's fire in Congress, a few live coals had fallen into a wood box next to their stove. Angie described the scene.

**In less time than it takes to describe what happened, townspeople went into action with a bucket brigade. Both the post office and the Collins' place burned to the ground. It was only through the valiant efforts of neighbors and my printer, Tom Kellis, that the printshop was saved. I salvaged a broken photographic plate of that fire.**

## The Ladies Bring Culture

Still a backwater town with no water, electricity, or other amenities such as local law enforcement, town government, library, or bank, Wickenburg looked like one gigantic trash dump. Fifty years of junk littered homes, streets, and vacant lots. As one of her first civic undertakings, Angie published a call for planning a town facelift.

Only a dozen women and one man, Dr. Fleming, showed up for this meeting. Because of the lack of interest on the part of the town's menfolk, the women decided to go ahead and fork rubbish into wagons by themselves. This plan shocked Dr. Fleming. He begged them not to set a date for the cleanup until he took the matter up with the chamber of commerce.

As a result, businesses closed on the day of the big cleanup. The whole town pitched in and carted away hundreds of loads of trash. As a reward from the grateful women, a huge picnic lunch was served at Baxter's Lumberyard.

Inspired by the success of this undertaking and their town's new appear-

Angela watches flames consume the Wickenburg post office on January 18, 1910. The Collins home, between the post office and the *Miner* building, had already burned to the ground.

ance, this core group of women discussed other ways in which refinement and culture might be brought to Wickenburg, a town with a reputation for brawling and disorderly conduct. Perhaps, the women suggested, if people had access to books, they might read more and lose some of their boorish ways. All agreed that their first goal should be a town library, but how could they convince the public of the importance of reading? The best way to do that, they decided, would be to act as role models themselves. They would form a reading club, and Angie would publicize their progress in the paper and encourage everyone to join the group.

The ladies couldn't have chosen a more controversial or ambitious book for their first selection. How they managed to come up with Markham's *History of the Races* is anyone's guess. It's hard to imagine that anyone would be enticed to join a group that held weekly discussions and monthly "test parties" over the contents of a book, but join they did. Angie trumpeted this "fun" on the front page of the *Miner*, and the reading club expanded into the Wickenburg Civic Association.

The drive for a town library got under way with, of course, Angie as the chairman. Each month she appointed a new finance chairman, who, in turn, selected a new committee of fund-raisers. These committees competed with each other for the distinction of raising the most money. They held dances, ice cream socials, box lunches, chicken pie dinners, and tamale dinners. In this way, practically everyone in town was working toward the goal of a library.

The library committee gave George Root twelve hundred dollars for the option of buying his old building on Railroad Street between the post office and a restaurant and saloon. Some people objected to the library being so close to the noisy railroad; others felt that the building's central location and modest cost outweighed this drawback. E. S. Jones, manager of the Brayton Commercial Company, was made legal trustee to hold title to the property, and work began on shelves and tables. People brought books from home, and a committee solicited donations from businesses and other sources. Mrs. Jennings, the leading solicitor, received money or books from Sears Roebuck, Montgomery Ward, and many Phoenix and Prescott business concerns. A man at Castle Hot Springs donated a wonderful collection of books from his own library. Soon more than two thousand books lined the shelves and were being catalogued by the librarians, Gen and Veva Murphy.

Locals and visitors alike enjoyed dropping into the quiet reading room of the new library to read, to rest, or to hold meetings, but it didn't remain in existence for long. One restroom between the saloon and the library served both establishments. A drunk using this facility dropped a lighted cigarette or match into a trash can, sending the efforts of the civic association up in flames. It would be several years before the town built another library with the help of Angie's future brother-in-law.

## Welcome, Brother-in-Law

Pattie, the only Hutchinson sister to remain unwed, left her job with the Santa Fe Railroad to live with her mother in Wickenburg. This attractive and financially independent thirty-eight-year-old woman took a job as stenographer for Francis Xavier O'Brien's Interior Mining and Trust Company on Center Street. So far, Pattie had managed to spurn the advances of just about every man she met, so no eyebrows were raised when she left Wickenburg for a vacation in New York City. Francis Xavier O'Brien, known as F.X., took her to the train station and dropped out of sight for a week or so.

Meanwhile, several Interior stockholders arrived unexpectedly. They raised a commotion because they couldn't find either F.X. or the company's accountant, Fred Mueller. When Mueller heard about these disgruntled investors, he sent word to F.X. to return to Wickenburg.

At midnight a short time later, Angie heard a knock at the door and a voice calling, "I have a message from Pattie."

Fearing something terrible had happened to her sister, she hurriedly opened the door. There stood F. X. O'Brien, dapper as usual, smiling through his carefully trimmed Vandyke beard, and wrapped in an expensive cloak to cover the hook that replaced his missing hand. A black-and-white Airedale sat at his heels.

"Don't worry," F.X. said, noting the look of concern on Angie's face. "Pattie is fine. She sent me to tell you that she has married."

Angie's eyes widened in amazement. Surely, her practical sister wouldn't have eloped. "Tell me quick! Who did she marry and what kind of person is he?"

F.X. had a mischievous twinkle in his eye. "Well, I think he's a pretty decent fellow and fairly well-off. His name is Francis Xavier O'Brien."

Francis Xavier (F.X.)
O'Brien in the early 1900s.

Angie laughed in relief. "Welcome, Brother!"

Even though Angie knew that F.X. was about the wealthiest and most mysterious figure in Wickenburg, she had always liked him. He had worked with her to clean up the town and seemed to be on the side of fairness and decency in every controversy.

A whole book could be written about F.X. even before he married Pattie at the age of fifty-nine. In 1877, he and James Mahoney discovered the Gold Bar Mine, about fifteen miles northeast of Wickenburg in the Black Rock Mining District, where William and J.K. later worked their claim. F.X. organized the Interior Mining and Trust Company, returned to Wickenburg in 1888, hired a large force of miners, and built a reduction plant at the mine. For years, he shipped gold bars to Phoenix that were worth twenty-five to thirty thousand dollars apiece. As his fortunes increased, he bought John Wisdom's eighty-acre homestead and Henry Wickenburg's place southeast of town along the Hassayampa. There, he experimented with different varieties of fruit and nut trees, trying to discover which kinds were best suited to conditions along the river. He called this ranch La Testa and transformed an old adobe house into a lovely hacienda with palm trees, rosebushes, and goldfish ponds. F.X. believed in gracious living.

The news of Pattie and F.X.'s marriage elicited different reactions from members of the Hutchinson family. Sarah was furious. F.X. was old enough

The Gold Bar Mine crew in the early 1900s. James Mahoney and F.X. stand at far left. The building still remains at its location twelve miles east of Wickenburg.

to be Pattie's father, and she didn't like the fact that he'd been married before. Gen usually sided with her mother on family matters, but Addie tried to stay neutral. However, it was Monica and her husband, William Bell, who were most stunned by the news. Many years earlier, Dr. Bell had amputated F.X.'s hand in Leadville, Colorado.

As it happened, Dr. Bell, a young surgeon, had returned from the Civil War to find his wife expecting another man's baby. Overwhelmed with grief and anger, he took off, wandering aimlessly westward in an effort to overcome his heartache. In the turbulent mining town of Leadville, he took a room at the posh Board of Trade Club, where gentlemen could eat, sleep, and play poker or billiards. Just down the street, Doc Holliday dealt faro at the Monarch Saloon.

One evening, a drunken patron lost heavily at the poker table and accused the club's proprietor, F. X. O'Brien, of running a crooked house. Whether F.X. had actually been at the poker table or whether he had tried to evict the man is unknown. Whatever the circumstances, this irate patron pointed his pistol at F.X., saying, "You may have my money, but you'll never work again." With that, he shot F.X. in the lower right arm at close range.

Dr. Bell amputated F.X.'s shattered arm right there on the poker table, using only whiskey as an anesthetic. He remained to care for F.X. until recovery was certain.

The two men journeyed to Arizona separately and coincidentally married sisters in the same family.

From that point on, relationships within Angie's family began deteriorating. One day Sarah came to Angie in a rage, claiming that F.X. was encroaching on her property. "I saw the location pit with my very own eyes, and Mr. Holland agrees it is on my ground!"

F.X. had hired Mr. Holland to dig a prospect pit on ground that adjoined Sarah's lot. Both Pattie and Angie believed that Holland was deliberately trying to foment trouble by digging this hole in a location to ensure dispute. Nothing could persuade Sarah that the prospect was not on her lot. Given the jealousies already existing toward F.X. because of his wealth, his acquisition of property, and the very nature of the man, this dispute reverberated throughout the entire town.

Boundary disputes over Henry Wickenburg's lots were very common. When Henry Wickenburg filed his town site adjacent to his 160-acre homestead just below Valentine Street in the 1870s, surveyors platted and recorded boundary lines according to territorial law. These lines were described in metes and bounds, with some so-called stable object as the starting point, more often than not nothing more than a boulder, easily displaced over the years. Many legitimate owners found themselves unable to obtain clear title to the 25- by 140-foot lots they had bought from Henry. Enter the Hollands, as inheritors of Henry's property, who jumped on the situation, charging property owners up to 150 dollars for quitclaim deeds to lots the owners had bought for ten dollars.

In addition, the Hollands were bringing suit against F.X. for diverting water from the Hassayampa across some of these lots with unclear titles, lots that belonged to F.X.'s friends. This mutual canal watered their gardens and trees as well. Despairing of all the legal entanglements and unable to come up with the money for quitclaims, these property owners agreed to sell their lots to F.X. if he would take on the fight with the Hollands. The case came to court as a double lawsuit between the Hollands and F.X.

Angie published an article about this squabble in the *Miner*, an article with two distinctions. First, it may have begun with the longest opening sentence in journalism history, and second, it is the only surviving remnant of the *Wickenburg Miner* other than two issues of the paper that found their way into the Sharlot Hall Museum in Prescott. This yellowed remnant, dated in March of 1909, showed Angie using her paper as a soapbox.

**We notice by the court proceedings in Phoenix this week that F.X. O'Brien has brought suit against Helene Holland and husband to quiet title to two pieces of ground in this town, one being known as the Case lot, and the other, the Contreras lot, both of which were purchased by Mr. O'Brien, and deeds to which were secured from Henry W. Wickenburg, the original owner, by Case and Contreras, and now the validity of the titles are being attacked by the present possessors of the Wickenburg estate, Helene Holland and husband, and the matter is assuming a serious phase for every property owner in town. If the affidavits recently made by these people in connection with the cases here mentioned is a criterion of their character, it behooves the property owners to be on their guard against their questionable and mysterious ways. People who take the law into their own hands and try to gain a point by threatening the lives of people and bulldozing in order to blackmail, will find that the time when such methods were in vogue have vanished into the distant past. At present,**

**no good citizen who recognizes the law as supreme would tolerate such modes
of procedure.**

The Hollands lost the court case to F.X., appealed the decision, lost again,
and had to pay all the court costs. Much to Sarah's distress, the Hollands sold
all their remaining property to F.X. and left town. F.X.'s extensive holdings
now surrounded Sarah's lot.

### A Desert Newspaper Syndicate

During the 1909 through 1912 era, Angie received travel scrip from the Santa
Fe Railroad in exchange for advertising and printing. She used this travel entitlement for a cursory trip to the little mining settlements growing up along
the new Santa Fe line that ran from Phoenix through Wickenburg to Parker
and on to the Colorado River. Each community wanted a newspaper of its
own to boost civic pride and boom mining developments in its region.

Since it wasn't feasible to put a printing plant in each town, Angie agreed
to print a nicely cast front page for each community. This front page would
carry local news and advertising and be attached to the regular Wickenburg
newspaper. She called this syndicate her "desert newspaper chain," and it included the *Eagle's Eye* at Aguila, the *Wenden News*, and the *Swansea Times*.
For a while, she even printed Dick Wick Hall's *Salome Sun*. In each town, she
established a correspondent with whom she visited weekly for news. Since
she couldn't make all these rounds in one day, she bought a lot in Bouse, where
the branch line to Swansea joined the Santa Fe. There, she put up a tent house
for overnight stays.

The papers in her desert newspaper chain mainly carried news about mining developments. For a time it looked as though all of northern Yuma County
would be great gold country. With the building of the railroad, George Mitch-
ell and T. J. Carrigan brought all the district's gold claims around Bouse into
the Clara Consolidated Gold and Copper Mining Company. Swansea (named
for Swansea, Wales, a great copper smelting center) had 750 residents. It was
through Father Quitu of Prescott, one of Clara Consolidated's most enthusi-
astic supporters, that the *Miner* acquired a number of subscribers in France,
all stockholders in the Clara Consolidated.

Excitement surrounded a discovery in the Lost Mine District east of Bouse
when Frank Heine found a rich ledge showing coarse gold that assayed at 150

dollars a ton. Local legend told of a lone prospector who had staked claims in the area many years before. As the story went, this prospector's horses ran off during a great dust storm. Soon out of food and water, the old man started across the desert on foot and lost his way. He was found wandering far from his claim and didn't live long. This recent discovery by Heine fit the description and location of the old prospector's claim.

Angie remembered some of the developments and promoters associated with this period.

**Dick Wick Hall seemed to have a magic touch for locating glory holes showing picture gold, but it all petered out before long. In Aguila, J.C. Denton promoted the Pay Car Mines, and the Osborne properties looked promising. Otis Young was the moving spirit for a town site at Wenden. The King of Arizona Mines, much in the limelight at the time, experienced a dimming of its glory when ore values declined. The company ceased operations and the town of Kofa became uninhabited and forgotten.**

**Gold fever subsided after many prospectors found that visible gold in mineralized rocks in this reddish-colored desert was only tiny, thin flakes with too much barren rock to pay for treatment.**

**All those old town sites were much the same amid the all-encompassing desert, a desert that blooms in glorious tints in a wet spring but gets rather discouraging during the dry season.**

## Saloonkeepers Laugh as Town Votes Dry

Before 1910 Wickenburg seemed to enjoy living up to its reputation as the toughest town in Arizona. Fifteen saloons and their painted ladies served a town of only five hundred people. Most married women didn't object to their husbands dropping in for a cold one to catch up on the latest, but when the number of corseted beauties masquerading as pianists mushroomed, the good wives began to take notice. These painted ladies paraded about town, dragging their satin trains through the dirt as they refereed street brawls and rendered the air with profanities. "Respectable women" often became the targets of insult on their errands to the meat market or post office.

Louie and Billy began to take an interest in this life on the streets. "What makes these ladies use such bad words?" Billy asked his mother.

Time for an object lesson, Angie decided. "Well, dear, I would say the poor creatures probably lost their mamas when they were young and had no one to teach them better, or maybe this dreadful behavior comes from taking that first drink of whiskey when they were young and innocent."

The whole town rocked with riotous merriment after payday at the mines and ranches. Morning light found many a moribund reveler prostrate on the street or sidewalk. Angie wrote that rolling these drunks was a quick way for transients to line their pockets on the way to the next town. "No man's pocketbook was safe if he drank too much."

Although the town was not yet incorporated, there was a constable and a justice of the peace. Angie talked to the constable about a law that prohibited saloons from harboring women on a permanent basis.

"You must catch the prostitutes in the act and swear out a warrant," the constable told her. "Otherwise, if the case comes to trial and you can't prove anything, you have to pay the court expenses out of your own pocket. I've secured depositions from numerous witnesses, but when the time comes to testify, they either disappear or retract their statements. No one wants to get mixed up in a fight with the saloonkeepers."

Angie squared off at these conditions of vice and aimed both barrels of the *Miner* at the saloon owners. Her articles occasioned a visit to her office by the rotund Mr. Kelly, who had known her mother and father in Virginia City. "I feel at liberty to give you some advice since I've known you for so long. Be a good girl, lay off the saloons, and keep this stuff out of the paper. I'd hate to see either you or your printing plant come to any harm. This ain't nuthin' for a lady to be writing about anyway."

"Thanks, Dad," Angie replied. "I promise not to write anything that shouldn't be said." As soon as Mr. Kelly left, Angie wheeled around to her typewriter and wrote an editorial about the visit and the threat.

When this editorial hit the streets, pandemonium broke out, with fistfights between Angie's detractors and defenders and further threats to the printing plant.

At this same time, the Women's Christian Temperance Union had begun a campaign to dry up Maricopa County. Any community could vote itself dry if it could muster a majority of votes. The WCTU had set up camp in Wickenburg and was in the process of surveying the town to determine if such a local-option election might be feasible.

This survey revealed that some residents were violently opposed to what they called "persecution of legitimate businesses." These residents pointed out that saloons were the town's biggest taxpayers and gave more aid to schools and charities than did any other business. Others said they didn't really care what happened to the saloons and wouldn't be sorry if such establishments were driven out of business. Several of the town's most notorious drunks testified that whiskey had ruined their lives and promised to vote dry if it came to an election. For the most part, however, people held strong sentiments against the rowdy behavior that accompanied the whiskey business. Surprised and reassured by the results of this survey, the WCTU set about petitioning the board of supervisors for a local-option election in Wickenburg.

Meanwhile, new construction began springing to life just beyond the Yavapai County line to the north, where the road to Congress passed between the riverbank and some steep hills. Building activity was evident, too, at Dad Rigg's place, which spanned the road to Phoenix and mining camps to the east. "Ahh, yes," the old-timers said. "A building spurt. A sure sign our town is growing." However, most residents were too busy campaigning for the election to think of much else.

On election day, the town hummed with a red-hot rivalry about who could get the most voters to the polls regardless of anyone's position on the issue. Even some of the town's old sots, with "dry" banners posted on their wagons, provided transportation. When the "drys" spotted Al Everts and Felipe Garcia, two prominent saloon proprietors, hauling anti-saloon people to the polls in their cars, they interpreted this courtesy to mean that the "wets" thought their side was invincible.

It didn't take long to count the votes. Three people out of every four voted to abolish the saloons. This was the largest majority of any precinct in Maricopa County. Angie said it seemed a bit peculiar that there were fewer "wet" votes than the number of saloons in the town. Instead of the predictable fistfights and black eyes that usually accompanied the outcome of an election, the "wets" smiled and shook hands with the leaders of the opposition. This unexpected streak of gentility caught the "drys" off guard. "Did you ever expect these saloon owners to be such good sports?" they remarked wonderingly to each other.

That night, the town celebrated its liberation from strong drink with one long, last bash.

With the saloons boarded up, peace and calm prevailed. No longer did raucous laughter, song, and epithets ring through the streets of Wickenburg. Youngsters quit waiting for the next street brawl to occur, and respectable women went about their errands without fear of harassment. But before the town could fully make the transition into a wholesome, family-friendly environment, a familiar sight returned.

At first, it was just a couple of inebriates found lying on sidewalks or vacant lots, but each morning their numbers increased. "Where are they getting their corn juice now?" people asked each other. Angie explained what happened.

**Little did the "drys" dream they had won but a pyrrhic victory. While the "wets" smiled their way through the election, they were opening new saloons at sites that controlled traffic from all directions just across the Maricopa County lines.**

Safely beyond the jurisdiction of the local-option district, these new saloons had been built just over the line in Yavapai County. But the "wets" made two mistakes. One was underestimating the power of a newspaper, and the other was carting their drunks into town each night and piling them in places to provoke the most "drys."

The day of reckoning came when the territorial legislature enacted a law prohibiting the operation of any roadhouse or the selling of liquor within three miles of the boundary line of any county that had adopted prohibition laws.

Thus Angie had used her "pig in a poke" as a potent instrument to bring order and respectability to the town of Wickenburg.

### The Old Town Gets Hot

It didn't take long for the animosity between Sarah and F.X. to precipitate into a town feud. F.X. was called "Foxy" behind his back. Angie took a hand in the fray by writing editorials commending F.X. for his civic-mindedness when he planted trees along the street in front of the Interior office, donated time and money to help build a Catholic church, and spearheaded innumerable other town projects. An anti-O'Brien faction emerged from this feud and spilled over into the town council elections after Wickenburg voted to incorporate.

In the first town election, Henry Cowell became mayor and R. W. Baxter, Felipe Garcia, C. H. Widmeyer, and John Bachtiger became councilmen. A

1975 publication, *The Right Side Up Town on the Upside Down River*, stated, "Politics in town between the People's Party and the Citizen's Party developed into a situation which caused the Election of 1910 to be invalidated and those previously elected to be reinstated by the Governor of the Territory." Could these two parties have been the outgrowth of pro- and anti-F.X. factions?

In her later years as a member of the Phoenix branch of the American Pen Women's Association, Angie wrote a short story that sheds light on what she thought was going on in the town. In it, she clearly fantasized about how a male editor might have handled a skirmish with an outraged citizen.

### THE COUNTRY EDITOR

John Righter, publisher, news reporter, ad man, janitor, and everything else that falls to the lot of a country editor, sat at his desk, grinding out editorials for the *Town Crier*. Today's editorial was a commendation for one of the town's leading citizens, Old Foxy, who had planted rows of trees along the streets in front of his various town properties.

Day after day, Editor John had listened to his college chum, Dan Cullen, criticize Old Foxy. Today, he dreaded going out on his news gathering rounds because he knew where he would find Dan and his pal, the town doctor. They would be in Dan's office, where they spent hours each day diagnosing the town's ills, their feet cocked on the desk, and their fingers on all the sore spots in town.

Just the other day, Dan had told Editor John that he and the doctor wanted the previous council elections declared illegal so they could put Old Foxy in his place. Now John only hoped that he would have an opportunity to spare his likable, but arrogant, old college friend from the humiliation that would likely befall him if he continued on his course of trying to become a political boss in the town.

John had barely finished reading over his editorial when Dan, his face redder than usual from haste and excitement, came bursting in with some important news. "I'm going to do it, John! I'm going to run for mayor! We'll get the last election overturned and have a new vote for town council. Doc will be alderman and with Jake on the board, I can just see Old Foxy wilt. Come on, John, be honest and tell me how this strikes you."

"It strikes me as asinine, Dan. You'll get yourself in trouble with your dictatorial attitude. What's wrong with the present council anyway?"

"We're fed up with this one gang rule. All they do is dance to Old Foxy's tune. I'm for having another election and putting in some real men. Doc and I already have our nominating petitions out. Much as I hate the thought, I'll kiss every dirty-faced baby in town and shake hands with the leaders of the Mexican population, even the garbage man if I have to. Can I count on you to give me a good write up and a promise of your support, old pal?"

"Can't do it, Dan, and I'd advise you not to attempt this overturn of the last election. You're doing it for all the wrong reasons."

A short comment about Dan's visit appeared in the next issue of the *Crier*. It said, "Col. Daniel Cullen, one of our leading citizens, has announced his determination to run for the office of mayor despite the advice of a friend who believes Dan's influence could be used to much better advantage in the role of a constructive citizen."

With fists clenched and blood in his eye, Dan strode into the *Crier* office shouting at John, "You double crossed me, you dirty rat! I'll teach you to handle my name with care!" With that, he reached across John's desk and grabbed him by the hair. Just as he was about to pull him across the desk, he found himself looking into the muzzle of a Colt 45.

Dan's red face paled, and he stepped back.

The rest of the story had to do with Dan's disillusionment at the outcome of the election even though practically everyone in town had promised to vote for him. "People are just natural born liars," Dan confided to the editor after the friendship was repaired. "I still can't get over the shock of you pointing a gun at me. You, of all people! But it did help bring me to my senses."

Angie ended the story with editor John's wondering reply. "I didn't realize how efficacious an empty gun could be." She must have wished she could have resorted to such tactics herself.

Adding to the difficulties of this period, Sarah passed away in 1912. Strangely, Angie made no note of her mother's death. We can only guess that differences of opinion over F.X. and church doctrine led to an ever-widening schism between the Hutchinson women and their mother. Pattie's daughter once told me that as a child growing up in Wickenburg she did not realize that the tiny old lady who lived in a house she passed each day on her way to school was her own grandmother.

The fight between the opposing parties for control of the town council clearly marked a turning point in Angie's love affair with Wickenburg.

# FIVE

## ∼ An Unholy Alliance

"THE ENMITY that's tearing this place apart isn't about what's best for the town," Angie told her printer, Ed Whalen. "It's just a power struggle between individuals. I have close friends and family on both sides of this town council fiasco, and they all expect my support in the *Miner*. Whichever way I go, or even if I take no stand at all, I fear the upshot will be bad blood for years to come."

Ed studied his employer's drawn but still unwrinkled face. "Why don't you just leave town until this thing blows over and people cool off? I can manage here for a while."

"I've given that some thought, too, but it's a luxury I can't afford." Pensively poking a pencil into her upswept hair, Angie wondered out loud: "What if I took the job press, paper stock, and some type and set up a little temporary print shop in Phoenix? My boys are old enough to help. Louie is becoming quite the mechanic. He tore apart and put together an old railroad handcar while we were in Congress, and I'm having a hard time trying to keep him in school. If we established a little Hammer and Sons' print shop, I wouldn't have to take money out of the *Miner* account."

### An Air of Entitlement

In the summer of 1913, a middle-aged man, adrift in cigar smoke, strode into the Hammer and Sons print shop on North Fourth Street in Phoenix. He extended his hand to Angie. "Ted Healey is the name. We met a while back in Wickenburg, but you probably don't remember me. Ed Whalen told me I'd

Angela in her forties.

find you here. I'm the former publisher of the *Bulletin* in Cochise County, and I'm looking for a place to relocate."

Angie shook Ted's hand. "Where are you thinking of locating? As far as I know, most of the communities in Maricopa County already have well-established hometown newspapers."

"Well, I have some good friends in a little town in Pinal County — a place called Casa Grande. It's swarming with settlers taking out homestead claims on the desert."

"What do those settlers intend to do there? There's little water for farming."

"You're wrong about that. Agriculture is thriving in the Toltec District, southeast of Casa Grande. Growing big crops of lettuce and melons, I hear. They're having huge success pumping underground water."

Angie looked doubtful. "Windmills can only pump so far. I wouldn't want to depend on them to irrigate large fields."

"Naw, these new-fangled pumps nowadays can pump water clear from China. There's plenty of water in that desert."

"That's all well and good, but why are you telling me this?"

"Thought you might like to go into partnership with me to publish a newspaper in Casa Grande. You've got the printing equipment, and I've got the savvy to make it work."

"I'm sorry, Mr. Healey, but most of my equipment is still with the *Miner* in Wickenburg, where I intend to return in a year or so. Besides, I don't have the kind of money it takes to establish a new publication." As an afterthought, Angie added, "I thought Casa Grande already had a newspaper."

Healey blew a ring of smoke toward the ceiling. "Wrong again, Mrs. Hammer. Oh, there's some old rag there — the *Casa Grande Times* — but I'd hardly call it a paper. It's not even printed locally. If money is bothering you, I'll supply whatever we need for the start-up. After we get the paper launched, I'll take over and you can go back to Wickenburg." He winked at Angie. "Two newspapers would make you and the boys a handsome living. I'll be back tomorrow, and I won't take no for an answer."

Though normally accepting and charitable toward people, Angie found something disagreeable about Healey and his air of casual entitlement. Intuition told her to not get involved, but this wasn't the first time she'd heard about the farming development in the Casa Grande area. She was curious about that.

Ted returned the next day and thrust a train ticket into her hand, saying, "No commitment, whatsoever. Just go with me to size up the town and talk to people."

Angie agreed to the trip.

## That Miserable Uneasiness

In its youth, Casa Grande had boasted more saloons than its entire population put together. Now the town was patented (that is, the public lands were conveyed to the town's control), and dusty new roads angled off Main Street. Respectable business establishments replaced the old saloons. On the outskirts of town, a sea of white stretched into the distance — tent homes of new settlers unable to find other accommodations. Chartered railcars stood about in the railroad yard, cars that contained the household goods, farm implements, and, in some cases, livestock of these new arrivals. Although the town still supported railroaders and miners, it exuded a new air of purpose and activity. Angie was amazed at all the changes that had taken place in the town where she had first set foot on Arizona soil more than thirty years earlier.

Mr. McFate, a local realtor, toured the town with Angie and Ted. He introduced them to merchants along Main Street: the Armentas, the Cruzes, the Pearts, the Bennetts, and Nichols and McCondra. They talked with Mr. Tenney, the town's only police officer, and Gordon MacMurray, who owned a livery stable. Angie was surprised to find that the town had two hotels, the W. T. Day Hotel and the Minear, and both a Catholic and a Protestant church. Everyone she met seemed upbeat about Casa Grande's future and promised support to their newspaper.

Angie's attitude toward Ted Healey softened. He already knew a lot of people, and everything he said about the town squared with her impressions of it. Before the day ended, she and Ted shook hands on a partnership. They agreed to call their paper the *Bulletin* after the one Ted had published in Cochise County.

Ted promised, "This is a fifty-fifty partnership all the way. You supply the equipment, paper stock, and ink, and I'll kick in the money. Five hundred dollars to start, and I'll also pay the freight costs of having your equipment hauled down here."

Back in Phoenix, Angie described Casa Grande to Gen. "It's just what you've been looking for, a place for that boardinghouse you've always wanted and a place where you can raise cows and chickens and grow a vegetable garden. Who knows? If you move down there with me, maybe we'll find some land to homestead."

Gen was ready for a change. She and J.K. had been divorced for years. Veva had completed her nurse's training and was giving piano and voice lessons as a sideline. But Gen was skeptical about Angie's partnership. "Why, you hardly know the man. Don't you think you are being way too impulsive?"

Angie's uneasiness returned when she found that Ted couldn't drive a nail straight. He stood around giving orders while she, Gen, and the boys built crates for shipping the print shop's machinery and supplies. Behind his back, the boys made faces and shook their heads in disgust. They couldn't believe that he didn't know how to use a hammer and saw. Angie felt like telling him to get lost and kept repeating to herself, "Get thee behind me, Satan."

After readying the crates for shipment, Angie and Ted returned to Casa Grande only to find not a single building or warehouse in which they could set up shop. Mr. McFate came to their rescue. "Until something more suitable turns up, you're welcome to use the back office in my building if your machinery will fit. It's pretty small."

McFate had better news about a residential property for Angie and Gen. The Weavers had just vacated a house belonging to Mr. Peart. "It's close to the railroad, but it has the only bathtub in town."

Angie perked up when she heard that and asked if the property had its own well.

"No," replied Mr. McFate, "the water comes from the railroad storage tank close by. It had a well at one time that caved in on some poor guy who went down to repair it. Now people claim an apparition hangs around the well. Hope you're not scared of ghosts."

Gen liked the Weaver House with its covered porch and large fenced-in backyard, a fine place to keep a cow and chickens and have a garden. When Angie told her about the apparition, she laughed. "If I run into that ghost, I'll tell it to go jump in the well."

Ted invited himself to be Gen's first boarder. "It will be a few weeks before I can pay you. I have money coming in, but I'm so broke right now that I had to hit up Angie for money to buy cigars."

Angie's suspicions deepened when she heard this. Ted hadn't mentioned the five hundred dollars he'd promised her, and the crates of machinery were highly visible on the depot platform. Angie told Gen, "I'm not going to say anything to him, and we'll just see how long it takes him to admit he can't pay the freight."

The waiting game continued for two days until Angie could stand it no longer and confronted Ted. "How long are you going to pretend that you don't know the machinery has arrived?"

"Okay, Angie, let me explain the position I'm in. You see, some of my associates here in town promised financial backing for the newspaper. So far, they haven't come through, but believe me, I'll pay back every cent that I owe you. You just have to trust me."

Angie was incredulous. "Why haven't you told me this before? Who are these associates of yours?"

"It makes no difference who they are, since they haven't come up with any money yet. In six months we'll be the biggest newspaper in Pinal County. We'll get the government printing contracts away from the *Blade-Tribune* in Florence, and, with all the land transactions going on around here, we'll be on easy street. Right now, we have to get the *Bulletin* up and running."

Angie didn't know how to respond. She was angry with Ted but even more upset with herself for getting into this situation in the first place. Her first impulse must have been to go directly to the depot and have the equipment shipped back to Phoenix, but she was in too far to turn back. Marvin and Bill were in school, and Gen was settled comfortably into the Weaver House, preparing to serve home-cooked meals to the public. Angie ended up writing a check on the *Miner* account to pay the freight charges. For now, she decided, she would keep the peace with her partner.

With the machinery crammed into McFate's tiny back room, Angie had just begun printing an order of cards on the Pearl job press when Billy released his cat from the cage in which it had been shipped. The frightened animal tore blindly into the revolving wheel of the press, splattering blood and fur across card stock and equipment. Angie spent the rest of the day taping the cat's broken ribs, cleaning up blood, and trying to placate both the cat and its master. So went life with youngsters in a print shop.

Ted, a well-seasoned printer, spent as little time as possible in the shop. He would go out soliciting or delivering printing orders while Angie did the layouts and printing. When he collected money for a job she had printed, he would come back, count out the proceeds, and give her exactly half. Not once did he acknowledge the use of her supplies, paper stock, and equipment. Some partnership! Angie bit her tongue and waited.

### Handsome Prince of the Desert

Ted dumped a stack of mail and newspapers on Angie's desk one morning. He pointed to a brochure, made a few derogatory comments about it, and left the room. Angie looked over this brochure with interest. Under a man's handsome face, the caption read: "The Prince of the Desert, State Senator J. F. Brown, the Busiest and Best Loved Man in Arizona." A write-up praised the settlers of Casa Grande and ended with these eloquent words: "Like the ancient Toltecs, they [the settlers] need to put in their irrigation canal before they can reap the bounteous harvests that lie latent in the soil. The story of their long early struggles, leading to the founding of the Casa Grande Valley Water Users Association, is a record of real inspiration."

Why had this brochure so upset her partner? Angie wondered. She knew that the highly respected Senator Brown was Southern Pacific's chief telegraph operator, but she knew nothing about the Casa Grande Water Users Association. She tucked that piece of information away for future investigation.

The first edition of the *Bulletin* carried the headline "Our Famous Valley of the Casa Grande" and made its debut on September 11, 1913. A little blurb next to the masthead stated, "An Ocean of Pure Water at a Shallow Depth." A front-page story compared the valley's climate and fertility to the Nile Valley in Egypt. Both Angie and Ted knew the success of the *Bulletin* depended on Casa Grande's future in agriculture.

Many factors had contributed to the flurry of homesteaders arriving daily to seek their share of the American dream. Government-subsidized railroads had spent millions of dollars luring settlers into westward expansion, and the Desert Land Act of 1877 allowed 640 acres to an individual if the land could be irrigated within three years. That, combined with Pinal County's shallow water table and improvements in pumping equipment, brought scores of homestead entrymen from across the nation to try to develop farms in the arid desert. Land promoters had already bought up large tracts of valley acreage and placed ads in periodicals such as *Sunset Magazine* to further entice settlement. Casa Grande called its growing number of tent houses the "White City."

Angie paid a call to Senator John Fred Brown, taking with her the brochure that Ted didn't like. John Fred made a wry face when he saw it. "I'm afraid the women who put that leaflet together got a little carried away. It sure hasn't helped my standing with the men around here."

Cordially, John Fred answered her questions about the water users group and their efforts to build the Casa Grande–Florence canal. "Since we can't depend on rainfall, we have to bring water from the Gila River for the homesteaders, just like the ancient Hohokam Indians once did. But right now, there's a bunch up in Florence who are fighting us all the way. They'd rather put up with periodic washouts than let Pinal's west-end settlers have any water."

"What happened to the old Florence Canal Company?"

"Well, the canal gets clogged up with sand and silt every year, but they won't give up on it. That canal has gone through a dozen owners, and every single one has gone belly-up. In 1911 we started the Casa Grande Water Users and petitioned the Reclamation Service to build a dam at the San Carlos site. Instead of waiting around for the government to make up its mind, we decided to go ahead and start building the canal ourselves."

"How far have you gotten with it?"

"Just a few miles. Right now, I'm still trying to get everyone behind the project. The holdouts are the ones who already have irrigated land and water rights. Our new Casa Grande Water Users' canal will run north of the Florence Canal for twenty-two miles and, like the old one, will end at Picacho Reservoir. It's projected to bring in enough water to irrigate seventy thousand acres. If we can all work together, we can make this happen. If we don't, God help us . . ."

Angie didn't want to take up any more of the senator's time, so she ended the interview. "Be assured, Mr. Brown, that the *Bulletin* will publicize the worthy efforts of the water users group, and I hope you will lend your support to the paper. I promise I will never misrepresent you."

John Fred thanked her for her interest and wished her a good day but said nothing about supporting the *Bulletin*.

Angie hurried back to the office to tell Ted about the visit. "You've got to meet Mr. Brown. He's very personable and willing to share information about what's going on with the water users, but he sure clammed up when I talked about the *Bulletin*. I wonder why?"

Ted snorted. "So you met the irresistible prince of the desert, huh? Stay away from that man before he turns your head like he's done with the rest of the women around here. Our farmers are doing just fine pumping groundwater or paying for water provided by canal companies. We don't need your prince of the desert and his far-off pie in the sky scheme of bringing gravity-fed water clear from the Gila." He pounded his fist on the desk. "Our settlers need water now!"

The next few issues of the *Bulletin* boasted farms under development and carried pictures of water gushing forth from pumps. Articles gave statistics on the wells—how far to water, whether dug by hand or drilled, the kind of pump and engines used, and how many gallons of water per minute. Sheriff Tenney's well was hand dug, but he still got up to five hundred gallons per minute. Not a word was printed about the water users association or much of anything else going on in the community until Angie insisted that she write a front-page story about the new high school under construction.

Gen had been collecting back copies of the *Casa Grande Times*. To their surprise, both Angie and Gen found the paper's news coverage well balanced. It was definitely not the old rag that Ted made it out to be. In an April 1912 edition, Angie read that the attorneys for Charles Sligh and Frank Jewel of Florence were asking the secretary of the interior not to reject their client's application to use the Box Canyon on the Gila River for a dam site. The attorneys claimed that their clients had spent over eighty thousand dollars to help the San Carlos Indians develop the Box Canyon dam site for irrigation. The secretary refused to accept the application, calling Sligh and Jewel "promoters who expect to derive a profit from the sale of water rights."

What in the world was going on? Angie wondered. First she'd had to educate herself in mining, and now she had to figure out pump logs, water law, and all the confusing facets of government that were involved with the reclamation of land. Since she couldn't talk these things over with Ted, she would go directly to the man who had written the article—a Mr. J. R. Julian, the *Times* representative.

She found Mr. Julian at his real estate office and complimented him on his fine newspaper. True to the code of early editors welcoming a rival paper into town, Mr. Julian greeted Angie warmly and laughed when she told him that her partner had made the *Times* out to be a promotional sheet. "He's right, you know. In the beginning, John Fred Brown started the *Times* to promote the water users association, but we expanded it to meet the needs of the town."

Aha! Angie thought. That's why John Fred had changed the subject when she had asked him to support the *Bulletin*. She looked around Mr. Julian's office. "You have the *Times* printed in Tucson, don't you? I'm surprised that you haven't bought a press of your own."

"Printing is too much of a headache, and neither of us has the time. We'll leave that to you and Healey. Even though your partner began the *Bulletin* to oppose the work of the water users, you and I can be friends, can't we?"

Taken off guard by this question, Angie mumbled, "Yes, of course, but I — I — didn't know. Why would Ted oppose the water users?"

"There's all kinds of money from eastern capitalists floating around here — for land, for private water companies, and for promoting farm and pumping equipment. From the looks of your paper, I'd say Healey has cornered the latter market. He's a good Republican, so your paper should do well."

This information didn't sit well with Angie. "Republican? Not if I have anything to do with it! This partnership has been an unholy alliance from the very start! Mr. Julian, I can't thank you enough. If it wasn't for you, I'd still be in the dark."

As if on cue to the unfolding drama, the University of Arizona sent an agricultural demonstration train to Casa Grande to bring aid and information to settlers trying to farm and make homes in the desert. Angie went to one of the evening lectures and listened to the university's Dr. G. E. P. Smith talk about one of the many problems confronting the settlers — irrigation engineering. She wrote,

> He talked about the huge pumping plants now providing water for hundreds of acres of crops in the Toltec [Eloy] District and warned that the underground water supply was not unlimited. If pumping in the area were to be materially increased, the day would come when those cultivated fields would return to desert. He emphasized the necessity of supplementing the underground water supply with a flow of stored water from the proposed San Carlos Dam on the Gila River.

Greatly impressed with Dr. Smith's lecture, Angie wrote a strongly worded article about the groundwater situation and the dangers of overpumping.

When it was finished, she hung the article on a copy hook and went on about her business.

Ted looked over her article, wadded it up, and tossed it into the trash can.

When Angie returned and found her copy missing, she asked Ted if he'd seen it.

"Yep. I threw it away. I won't allow that kind of nonsense in my paper."

Angie's eyes flashed. "Your paper! Since when is this *your* paper?"

She found the wadded-up paper in the trash can, fished it out, and set the type for it herself. Over Ted's objections, she ran this article in the next issue of the paper. Then, to make matters worse, she ran a financial report for the water users association that Ted didn't want to publish. As Angie put it, "Thereafter, the firm sailed on troubled waters."

On an impulse of the moment, Angie stopped in to see Mr. Julian a few days later. After exchanging pleasantries, Mr. Julian said, "I hear that you're moving the *Bulletin* plant to the new chamber of commerce building."

"What? No one has said anything to me about moving. Where did you hear this?"

"Oh, the rumors about you and Ted are flying all over town. He says that you're a good little woman, but you don't know the first thing about running a newspaper. I guess Healey and his cronies want to get the *Bulletin* moved into a better location, so they will have more influence on the off side of the water and pump controversy."

Angie sank into the chair that Mr. Julian offered. "You are a true friend, but Ted's right. I am far too naïve when it comes to his shady business dealings." Suddenly, she jumped up. On her way out the door she yelled over her shoulder, "He thinks I'm a pushover, but I'm just Irish enough to do something about this plan being hatched behind my back!"

## The Partnership Comes Unglued

After supper that evening, a council of war was held at the Weaver House. Even Ben Woods, the new printer, said the partnership needed to be dissolved. "He doesn't treat you like a partner, Mrs. Hammer. If I owned that machinery, I wouldn't waste another minute. I'd call Gordon MacMurray at the livery stable right now. Gordon has a flatbed truck, and we could have that plant cleaned out in four hours."

The war council agreed to follow Ben's suggestion.

It was almost midnight when Angie told her confederates, "There's one more thing I need to do before I close this shop for the last time." She held up a paper with names and post office box numbers written on it. "Ted claims this little piece of paper is worth fifteen thousand dollars, so I'm leaving it to him. That's a fair trade, don't you think?" Carefully, she placed the *Bulletin*'s subscription list under a rock in the middle of the empty room.

A few blocks away, Gordon backed his truck, loaded with printing equipment and supplies, into his horse barn.

The next morning, Ben and the boys hid in the bushes around Mr. McFate's office to watch the fireworks. Ted didn't disappoint them.

Billy ran home to breathlessly report to his mother. "Maw, you should've seen his face. He comes swaggering down the sidewalk like this —" Billy put his shoulders back, pushed his belly forward, and pretended to puff on a cigar. He pantomimed Ted unlocking the door, blinking his eyes, and saying, "What the hell — ?"

Gen and Angie gave the boy's performance a round of applause.

"Did he find the subscription list?" Angie asked.

"Yeah, he stuffed it in his pocket and went out cussin' up a storm." Billy continued his charade.

Angie smoothed the boy's tangled hair affectionately and said, "You don't have to repeat those bad words. I think we better go see what Mr. MacMurray has to say this morning."

At the livery stable, Gordon put down his currycomb and hurried over. "Well, what happened? Did Mr. Healey go into shock?"

Billy did his swaggering, cigar-smoking act again.

Gordon laughed. "Is that how it happened?" He turned to Angie. "Mrs. Hammer, I need to use my truck. Where shall I unload your machinery?"

"I knew you were going to ask that. Can you let me have an hour or two to check around for an empty storeroom?"

She tramped all over town and couldn't find a single building available for lease. With her former ebullient mood a thing of the past, the dispirited woman returned to the livery stable to tell Gordon that he might as well begin crating up the machinery to send back to Phoenix.

Gordon looked stunned. "You mean you're going to give up on the *Bulletin*? I'll tell you what. I'll unload your machinery right here in this corral and frame in a building around it. I've been intending to build a warehouse here for a long time, and it will give me the incentive to get started. You can continue your printing while I build around the machinery."

A look of incredulity crossed Angie's face. "You mean print out here in the open?"

Billy clapped his hands. "Yes, sirree! The Hammers' new open-air printing establishment!"

Still skeptical about the idea, Angie asked Ben Wood what he thought about setting up the machinery on MacMurray's lot. How would he like printing in the open?

The idea appealed to Ben. "Better than printing in McFate's old dark back room. Plenty of light and ventilation!"

The Hammers' open-air print shop became an instant public attraction. Orders came in for flyers, business cards, and stationery, while intrigued townspeople stood around and watched the progress. Youngsters lined up to help hang freshly inked paper to dry and chase any newsprint scattered by wayward breezes.

### Birth of the *Dispatch*

Louie cranked out the first issue of the *Casa Grande Valley Dispatch* on January 1, 1914, a smudgy, tabloid-size, four-page paper. How it got printed under the existing weather conditions remains a mystery. A front-page report explained what was going on at the time:

> **With water and washouts on all sides of us, and no way to get in or out for several days, and five hundred additional people marooned here, there was some thought that the local food supply would run short. Our stores were so well stocked that the large numbers of extras did not make any difference, and everybody had all they wanted to eat and then some.**

After the first few editions, the title of another paper appeared under the *Dispatch*'s masthead. It now read "the *Casa Grande Valley Dispatch* and the *Casa Grande Times*." J. R. Julian and John Fred Brown had joined forces with Angie to consolidate their papers. Whether any money exchanged hands in this transaction remains unknown, but certainly the acquisition of another subscription list gave the *Dispatch* a financial and political boost. The combined papers sold for ten cents a copy or five cents in quantity.

By the end of February 1914, *Dispatch* headlines shouted, "Army Engineers Report Favorably on the San Carlos Project. Casa Grande Wins." The ensuing article explained the reason for celebration:

> **At a special jubilee meeting held by the Board of Trade [also known as the chamber of commerce], the people selected Mr. Peart as chairman of a committee to draft resolutions to our representatives in Washington and to the Army engineers. Mr. Peart selected Mrs. Hammer and J.R. Julian to assist on the committee, and some good, strong letters were immediately dispatched to the national capitol urging the immediate appropriation for the construction of the dam and expressing deep appreciation of the work of the Army engineers and our representatives.**

But the little town of Casa Grande still found itself with two newspapers! Ted Healey had managed to scrape together enough financing to buy machinery and continue publishing the *Bulletin*. No doubt, with Angie out of the picture, his benefactors had come forward more willingly.

Although the *Bulletin* also carried news of the army engineers and the water users association's push for construction of a dam on the Gila River, it clearly had a different agenda—to extol the virtues of irrigation by means of pumping. Angie often lamented the fact that Ted's paper got all the advertising for pump equipment and well drilling.

Despite everything, as each paper struggled for a foothold in the community, Angie maintained a sense of humor.

> **We carried on a crossfire of not so friendly words, much to the amusement of some of our readers and to the dismay of others. Our paper carried a little weekly feature entitled "Says Pat to Mike and Says Mike to Pat," which made fun of the whole situation between Healey and myself. I refrained from calling names or making charges against him, but he continued writing that his equipment had been stolen.**

While news about the war in Europe came over telegraphic lines at the Southern Pacific depot, a different kind of war began brewing at home, one that Angie knew only too well from her days in Wickenburg. The "wets" and the "drys" were at it again! Pinal County residents were soon to go to polling places to determine whether enforcement of a National Prohibition Act should be delayed. Arguments coalesced around the issue of individual freedom versus the social protection of families against the abuse of alcohol. Barbershops, saloons, and the columns of the *Dispatch* staged forums for discussion.

Again, the "drys" won the election and celebrated victory. Dr. H. A. Hughes led a band up and down the streets of Casa Grande in the rain to serenade downtown saloons. But Angie would soon regret the stand she took on Prohibition.

# SIX

## ∼ A Lovely Stretch of Desert

AFTER THE WILD SALT RIVER had been tamed by the construction of Roosevelt Dam in 1910, downstream desert lands blossomed with crops and mansions. Long-time residents lamented, "Why, I could have picked up that piece of worthless ground for nothing, and look at it now." Real estate mania increased with the introduction of better pumping systems, and people began taking second looks at available homestead lands.

Angie found her little piece of paradise on the eastern slopes of Casa Grande Mountain, a fine place for a home, farm, or retirement. She wrote, "It was a lovely stretch of desert. In the spring, purple ironwood trees bloomed around the base of the mountain with palo verdes adding a splash of yellow."

When Angie's brother-in-law, Dr. William Bell, came to Casa Grande in 1914 looking for land to homestead, she took him to this lovely stretch of desert. Dr. Bell wanted to raise Angora goats. As a practicing physician, he had found that allergic infants and children did very well on goat's milk, but they needed a reliable supply. The more he read about Angoras, the more he wanted to raise them, both for their milk and to market their lovely, silken hair used in mohair fabrics.

Dr. Bell, too, liked this lovely stretch of desert. He filed a homestead claim for 160 acres, drilled a well, and built a small frame house, a goat shed, and a large horse and hay-storage barn. He then surrounded 80 acres' worth of cholla, prickly pear, creosotebush, and hedgehog cactus with fencing. Into this lush native vegetation, he introduced a large herd of the Angoras and a Mexican goatherder.

After a few weeks of grazing, those aristocrats of the goat family looked like something akin to walking packrat nests. The goatherder quit and went back to Mexico.

Dr. Bell knew the venture was hopeless, and he talked about putting the improvements on his homestead up for sale. But Angie couldn't let go of this homestead dream so easily. Would he be willing to swap his interests for some property she owned in Peoria, Illinois? (Possibly this was part of Sarah's estate.) Dr. Bell readily agreed to the trade.

Angie and Gen knew that homesteading required the raising of crops and living on the land for five years, but what they hadn't really thought about was how Angie and the boys would make the twelve-mile round trip into town and back each day. This would entail renting a wagon and buying livestock. Gen said not to worry. She would see to the care of livestock and other ranch-related chores. But before they could close out the Weaver House, an occurrence at the printing plant delayed their impending move to the ranch.

By this time, Gordon MacMurray had erected an enclosure for the *Dispatch* office and plant, but this building still had a dirt floor and no door that locked. Angie noted,

> As far as protection from theft was concerned, we were no better off than we were on the vacant lot. But strange as it may seem, we suffered no loss until the disaster that aroused all the hell in me that one human may be entitled to.
>
> Some miscreant entered the newspaper plant at night, pushed pages of six-point [type] off the stone [worktable], scattered the type in the dirt and dismantled the office files.
>
> My Indian printer followed the vandal's footprints to right where I thought they would lead. I considered arrest but knew a lawsuit would cost more than resetting the type, so I decided that the perpetrator of this deed would have the punishment of his own conscience, if he had any.
>
> Since I couldn't make outright accusations, I wrote a torrid article about the deed and had the type for the legals reset in Phoenix. The *Dispatch* came out on time.

It may seem to a reader that this vandalism couldn't be as terrible as Angie made it out to be, but it's important to understand the situation. A big plum in the world of early newspapers had to do with county contracts for land office advertising, notices such as births, deaths, marriages, and bankruptcies, and homestead and mining claims. These contracts turned on political tides depending on the good will of the occupants of the capital in Phoenix or the county courthouse. The *Dispatch* at that time enjoyed a contract with Pinal County, which was its main means of remaining financially solvent.

Angie called these announcements "legals." By law, these legals had to run in four consecutive editions of the paper and remain filed in chronological order. If these conditions were not met—say, for instance, an edition of the paper came out without its legals—the printing contract would be awarded to the next closest paper in the county: in this case, the *Bulletin*.

Setting the six-point type for these announcements required extreme care and was very time consuming. Once set, the forms holding the type were stacked on the worktable to be used again the following week. Whoever committed this act of vandalism knew that Angie wouldn't have time to reset the legals before the *Dispatch*'s deadline. Her only way around this dilemma was to have the legals reset in one of the large printing plants in Phoenix or Tucson, a costly procedure. On top of this, Angie said that the guilty party had the nerve to pay her a visit to offer his sympathy. She didn't name the culprit in her writing, but it's not hard to guess who it might have been. After this setback, Angie, Gen, Veva, and the boys moved to the homestead, gradually settling into ranch life and those daily long buggy rides.

The boys raised a pet calf they named Flirt. They played matador with this calf, teaching it to paw the ground and butt heads with them. Each morning Flirt waited by the wagon for the boys to come out and play. Angie harbored a secret fear of bovines, stemming from a childhood spent on Nevada's open range, so when Flirt lowered its head, snorted, and charged at her, she didn't see any humor in the situation. While Flirt chased her screaming around the wagon, her sons laughed hysterically, knowing that Flirt wouldn't hurt their mother. What they didn't know was that her screams were real; she wasn't acting.

Except for their early morning workouts with Flirt, the boys soon lost interest in those long wagon rides to town. Angie had her hands full trying to keep Billy and Marvin, ages fifteen and twelve respectively, in school. She had given up on Louie, now seventeen. He had completed the eighth grade in Wickenburg and refused to continue on to high school. With his mechanical expertise, he made himself indispensable to the operation of the print shop. She consoled herself with the thought that, from years of setting type and working with words, Louie's spelling and vocabulary far exceeded that of the average high school student.

On May Day in 1914, Angie climbed aboard the wagon with a racing pulse after another invigorating chase by Flirt. Her blood pressure mounted even more as she and her sons noticed a rising black pall in the sky to the west over Casa Grande. This could mean only one thing—a fire in the town!

**How we tried to hurry that old horse and how vain it was! Nothing could make him accelerate his speed. The children and I had to possess our souls in patience.**

Entering the town with trepidation, they fully expected to find the printing plant razed by fire. Mercifully, it had escaped the conflagration, but just about all the buildings on Main Street had been leveled by the fire. The specter of those charred places of business with their salvaged furnishings lining the street would haunt Angie forever.

Angie described the cause of the fire in a *Dispatch* story entitled "Loss Estimated at Fifteen Thousand Dollars. Buildings to Be Replaced with Concrete and Adobe."

**Shortly after one o'clock Tuesday, the alarm of fire brought every resident of Casa Grande to the Main Street where flames were issuing from the roof of the Berlin Bakery and in an amazingly short time one block of business buildings were destroyed and a number of other places menaced. The fire started in the bakery when the oil fuel system under the ovens "back fired," shooting blazing oil out over the floor. The cook tried to put the fire out by dashing water over it, which only served to spread it.**

Even before the rubble of the Main Street fire had been cleared away, Joe Armenta burst into the *Dispatch* office one afternoon. "Mrs. Hammer! Mrs. Hammer! Come look!" He pointed toward a black cloud of smoke coming from behind Casa Grande Mountain. "It must be your home, Mrs. Hammer. It's the only thing out there that could cause that kind of smoke!"

Angie's knees went weak. The boys were out of school for the summer, and a friend of Gen's, Mrs. Cauldron, and her son Sam had been staying at the ranch as houseguests. Gen, Veva, and Mrs. Cauldron had left for Tucson that morning, leaving Sam and the boys alone.

Angie dashed for her buggy just as Maizie Fordham pulled up in her Model-T. "Get in! I'll have you there in no time!"

Maizie's Model-T seemed almost as slow as Angie's old nag. To Angie, it seemed like one continuous bad dream from which she couldn't awaken. By

William Carpenter, Judge Bennett, and Albert Furback survey damage of the Main Street fire.

the time the Model-T reached the trail to the ranch house, only a thin wisp of smoke marked their destination.

Once at the homestead, Angie counted the soot-charred faces of the young men standing around the pile of smoking embers that once was her house. She saw Billy, Louie, and Sam Cauldron, but not Marvin.

**You've heard stories about hearts standing still. Right then, I knew how it felt. I pictured my baby boy dead among the ashes.**

The boys descended on Angie, all talking at the same time. In the blur of the moment, she heard Marvin's name being repeated over and over and thought they were saying that Marvin hadn't survived. She sank to her knees, sobbing uncontrollably.

Louie, misreading his mother's devastation, tried to explain. "We had most of the stuff halfway out when the wind changed and the flames shot through the peak of the house like a blowtorch. It caught all the furniture on fire." He pointed to Mrs. Cauldron's charred trunk, a safe distance from the rest of the rubble. "That's all we managed to save."

Angie finally voiced her dreaded question. "What happened to Marvin?"

Louie shrugged. "I dunno. It was his turn to wash dishes. He built a fire in the stove and forgot about it." Louie whistled and, cupping his hands to his mouth, yelled, "Hey, baby boy, you can come out now and get your whuppin'."

A tow-headed boy emerged from the goat shed and shuffled toward his mother. "I didn't mean to do it, Maw."

Angie gathered the frightened boy into her arms. "Shh . . . I don't want to hear it. You're safe, and that's all that matters."

Casa Grande showered Angie and her family with sympathy, household items, and clothing. Maizie Fordham donated a Quick Meal kerosene stove and a used bedroom set from her hotel. The horses were moved out of their barn, and the family moved in with their meager furnishings. Gen and Veva got an apartment in town.

## A Tin Can Mansion

Before the tragedy of the fire, Clara Myers, one of Casa Grande's early "movers and shakers," had developed her tracts around town into lots. In exchange for advertising and printing services, she traded a lot in her new Myers' Addition to Angie. With Gen gone and few of the comforts of home remaining at the ranch, Angie and the boys began to toss around the idea of somehow using this lot.

Not wanting to put the ranch in jeopardy, they looked into the homestead laws and found that an entryman (or -woman) was permitted to live and work in town during the week as long as he or she resided at the homestead at all other times. That ended their discussion about whether a temporary residence in town would be allowed. Since they couldn't afford a tent house, what materials might they use for this temporary residence? The boys suggested tearing down the goat shed at the ranch and using its corrugated iron sheeting to construct a temporary shelter on the town lot.

Angie knew that her teenagers sometimes lacked good judgment, but she never doubted their ability to come up with a solution to a problem and carry through on it. She gave them the green light to dismantle the goat shed.

On the afternoon that Louie, Billy, and Marvin pulled into the town lot with their load of iron sheeting, a wild summer dust storm hit the valley. At the office, Angie couldn't get the image out of her head of what might happen to her boys with those flying sheets of iron swirling all about. She headed out into the blinding storm and churning debris to find them.

Find them she did—hunkered under a canvas sheet beneath the wagon. She had put herself in more peril than her boys faced. But, as she wrote in her memoirs, that incident proved to her that her sons possessed enough native intelligence that she didn't have to worry about their survival.

The boys nailed the metal panels from the goat shed onto a framework set up by a carpenter. This resulted in a twenty-by-forty-foot enclosure standing eight feet high, with a metal roof, no windows, no floor, no water, and, of course, no electricity. Then, to make the construction look like a giant tin of corned beef opened around the middle with a wind-up key, a three-foot opening for ventilation was cut midway around the house on three sides. Wire mesh covered this opening to keep out flying insects, and canvas flaps controlled the amount of sunlight that entered. Upon its completion, Louie declared the house a disgrace and said that he wouldn't live in it. But live in it he did, along with all manner of snakes, lizards, tarantulas, and scorpions.

When she went to cook supper one evening, Angie found an iridescent, green snake in her oven. She knew by the shape of its head that it wasn't venomous, so she allowed the snake to take its place within the family and share

rodent duty with Billy's cat. Gen came for a visit, and when the family returned that evening, she proudly announced her conquest of a horrible green
reptile. Despite the loss, life went on in the Tin Can Mansion.

Improvements to the mansion took place over time. First, it got a floor of
third-grade lumber that dropped its knotholes regularly. Billy's ill-fated cat,
the one that had been chewed up in the flywheel of the press, had a broken
leg that wouldn't heal. Angie said that the cat took charge of its own therapy
by lying with its broken leg poked down a knothole.

Before they installed the floor, the boys had dug a little root cellar to use
for food storage. A big rainstorm turned the whole floor of the house into a
lake, so they filled in the cellar and began brainstorming other ways to keep
food cool. With no ice available for an icebox, they came up with the idea of a
perforated pan that would consistently leak out just enough water to wet the
burlap around a wood-framed cold box. It worked beautifully and gave Angie
bragging rights about the brilliance of her sons.

However, the Tin Can Mansion's most lethal defect came from the lightning
that accompanied monsoon storms. Mansion occupants often found their
hair standing on end as fire flashed between the walls and the mesh screen of
the opening around the house. During the first such storm, Louie took his
mother's hand to lead her outside. "Come on, Maw, this place is too dangerous. Don't touch the screen or iron siding or you'll be electrocuted."

Another flash of lightning sent them scurrying back inside for cover. They
laughed nervously about whether they wanted to fry outside or inside.

The *Dispatch* continued carrying news about people, town activities, and
the progress of the water users association and its canal, but one persistent
rumor bothered Angie. She kept hearing that vegetable crops could not be
grown in desert soil during the first year of cultivation. One day she hitched
her team to a wagon to do a little investigative reporting. She would visit
some of the newly established farms in the area to check out the truth of
this rumor.

About ten miles southeast of Casa Grande, she came upon an unusual
sight—a man with a hand plow hitched to the back bumper of a Model-T
while his missus slowly drove the car back and forth across the dusty field.
Our reporter, delighted at this sight of ingenuity, stopped and took pictures.
Mr. and Mrs. Borree, the owners of this forty-acre tract, told her they intended
to plant potatoes and would keep her apprised of the progress of their crop.

From there, Angie visited the C. G. Houck Ranch. As proof of the success of their first year, the Houcks picked her a basket of produce from their garden — squash, carrots, and onions. Their watermelon vines promised a bumper crop but weren't quite ready for harvest.

When Angie wrote about her trip for the *Dispatch*, she described in great detail the dinner she had enjoyed with the Houcks: a bountiful feast of fried chicken and garden vegetables with whipped cream cake for dessert. Halfway through the whipped cream cake, there came the sound of an automobile engine grinding away in the distance. With few fences between Casa Grande and Florence, motorists took off in any direction, often bottoming out in gullies or getting hung up on boulders. Mr. Houck excused himself to go to the rescue, later returning with the stranded motorist to help finish off the whipped cream cake. With this description of her visit to new homesteads, Angie felt certain that the salacious rumor about first-year vegetable crops had been quelled.

Monsoon storms and early winter rains had transformed the desert and made weekends at the ranch more enjoyable. In December of 1914, Angie wrote a piece called "The Resurrection of the Dead," describing how her former forage crops of Sudan grass and feterita at the ranch sprang to life with the rain. She wrote that even the roselle plants, a kind of hibiscus that Gen had used for jellies and teas, now sported new blossoms. She ended her article with glowing comments about the ever-renewing cycles of nature and life.

On these weekend trips, Louie complained constantly about his mother remaining in the horse-and-buggy days while more progressive types had switched to automobiles. Clara Myers got wind of this and took Louie to her garage, where she stored a Sidewinder Reo that had belonged to her late husband. "It's just taking up space, and I'd like to get it out of here. Do you want it?"

Louie couldn't believe his good fortune. Afraid that Clara might change her mind, he immediately pushed the Sidewinder out of the garage and fiddled and cranked until it sputtered to life. He blissfully sailed along in his new chariot until a connecting rod blew through the crankcase. He had to push it the rest of the way home.

When it became apparent that Louie couldn't conquer the engine problems himself, mother and son weighed the pros and cons of the situation. After lengthy debate, they agreed to take the car to Hugh Wilson for diagnosis.

"Junk this heap," Hugh told them. "Repairs will cost seventy-five bucks, more than it's worth."

Angie couldn't bear the look of disappointment on her son's face. "I know this is crazy, but go ahead with the repairs. How about a trade for printing? I'll bet you can use some business cards or advertising."

They struck a deal, and Hugh went to work on the car. Louie never left Hugh's side. Even after the Reo was in top-notch shape, Louie continued to hang around the repair shop. Hugh realized he couldn't get rid of Louie, so he put the young man to work as a mechanic, along with his own son, Blinky. With misgivings, Angie watched Louie's interest turn from printing to the horseless carriage.

## The Claim Jumper

Before the widespread use of telephones, newspaper offices served as the communication hub of an entire community. If a newcomer wanted to locate someone, get directions, sell something, or find work, he or she headed for the newspaper office.

A man walked into the office one day and told Angie that he was a well driller looking for work. In the course of the conversation, Angie admitted that she'd like to have a well on her town lot, but she couldn't afford it. Mr. Kelly made it known that he was willing to barter. In trying to hit upon a suitable bartering item, Angie told Mr. Kelly about the fencing around the eighty acres at the homestead. His eyes lit up. Fencing was a scarce and expensive item in this part of the country where jackrabbits could lay waste to fields and gardens overnight. At this time of shallow water tables, Mr. Kelly eagerly agreed to dig a fifty-foot well in exchange for the fencing.

After finishing the well, Mr. Kelly disappeared, ostensibly to retrieve his prize, while Angie had a windmill and a water-holding tank installed for the well. Angie and the boys were surprised to find the fence still standing when they went to the ranch but supposed Mr. Kelly would eventually come for it.

At a time when town fathers had just begun discussing the possibility of a municipal waterworks, the Hammers' 1,500-gallon water tank set atop a twelve-foot tower represented a crowning achievement in the neighborhood. Angie invited all comers to help themselves to water.

Louie built a shower shed on the north end of the mansion and rigged it up with an oilcan attached to the end of a garden hose. After a hot summer day, what bliss to serenade the neighborhood while enjoying a refreshing shower! However, it wasn't long before the family began coming home to find their water tank empty. Every neighbor had put in a vegetable garden. Rather than take them to task, Angie installed a marker on the holding tank and asked her neighbors not to use water when the gauge reached a low point. All obliged, and even after the town had its own waterworks, the old windmill in front of the mansion continued pumping water for the neighborhood.

One Saturday morning, as the family approached their homestead in Louie's open-topped Reo, they almost literally lost their heads. Louie yelled, "Duck," and slammed on the brakes, while pushing down his mother's head. There, just at head height, a thin, almost invisible wire stretched across the driveway!

They stood around cursing the no-good so-and-so who would have done such a thing, until Marvin pointed toward the horse barn. "Look! Our stuff is all stacked outside!"

Stacked wasn't the right word. Maizie's bedroom set had been dragged out the door and all the Hammer belongings tossed on it in a heap. Someone else's furniture and possessions now occupied the horse barn. The air turned blue with invectives while the irate boys wasted no time in reversing the situation.

They spent the rest of the weekend trying to figure out who would have the nerve to invade their premises this way. Although they couldn't figure out the identity of the culprit, they did understand the motive. Someone intended to preempt their homestead claim by squatting on it.

Anxiously awaiting the return of this squatter, they finally had to give up and return to town after posting big "no trespassing" signs on the premises and wiring up the door.

The next weekend brought a repeat of the last, but this time, the Hammers' belongings were dumped even farther from the horse barn. The boys wanted to lie in wait for the trespasser while Angie returned to town, but she wouldn't hear of it.

Digging through an old dresser, Marvin came upon some letters addressed to the squatter—Mr. Kelly. Now the whole situation made sense. The well driller intended to take more than just the barbed-wire fence!

The upshot to this whole affair came when Mr. Kelly filed a trespassing complaint against Angie, probably thinking he could intimidate her into abandoning the homestead. There had been no written agreement about the bargain made for the well. When Angie cross-filed with a complaint against the driller, she knew it would be his word against hers in court.

Justice prevailed. The judge ruled in Angie's favor, saying that she had acted within her right of eminent domain. This female wasn't as vulnerable as the driller had first thought. He made sure that Angie's boys weren't around when he came to collect the fence and his belongings.

Angie still had three years to go before she could take full possession of the homestead. Like clockwork, she spent every weekend at the ranch with whichever one, two, or three of the boys wanted to go with her.

The violent squalls of wind and sand that blew around Casa Grande Mountain often sent the Hammers' horse-barn shelter into spasms of groans and shivers. When Angie told people in town about these storms, they would raise skeptical eyebrows. Why would her homestead have the kind of weather she described when six miles away, the town didn't have a drop of rain or a hint of wind? On the day that Angie reported that a whirlwind had leveled their home and left not even a horse stall standing, Casa Grande had not experienced any inclement weather. Everyone puzzled over this disaster, but all that Angie and the boys could do was pick up the pieces and move on. She noted,

**We gathered up what material we could find and built another house on a much smaller scale. Our forty-foot horse barn became a twenty-foot hastily erected shelter.**

What Angie called a whirlwind would be termed a microburst today. What Angie called a house we would call a thrown-together hut without a firm foundation. This puny shack was blown apart not once, not twice, but for three summers in a row. Each time, it was rebuilt with whatever wood could be salvaged, and each time, it became smaller.

Before undertaking the final rebuilding of the homestead house, the Hammers tried to analyze why their shelters kept blowing across the desert so readily. They finally concluded that they had been building right in the path of demon wind currents that traversed the mountain in certain directions. They chose a different location and anchored their ten-by-twelve-foot hut into the heart of a mesquite tree with the fervent hope that it would last until final proof could be made on the homestead.

Louie accompanied his mother on their last trip to the homestead before proving up on the land in late 1917 or early 1918. Angie's description of this event provides the full flavor of a plucky woman who quotes poetry in a hailstorm:

The fourth version of our architecture still stood. A fierce wind and hailstorm swept over the place while we huddled inside. Hail pounded so hard on our iron roof that I thought of those lines from the Balaklava. "Never since the days of Jesus roared so loud the Chersoneses." The cabin strained against the wind like a human clinging to Mother Earth for salvation. I expected to momentarily accompany the cabin in its final aerial flight over the desert.

The storm didn't last long. When it was over, our homestead was covered in a blanket of white hail that extended to within a mile or two of town. There had not been a single gust of wind or speck of hail in town that day.

## Under the Umbrella Tree

The downside of having three strapping sons was the occasional disagreements that led to fisticuffs. Headstrong Louie had long since positioned himself as the man of the family, while the gentler, more retiring Billy, two years Louie's junior, tried to keep the peace. Thirteen-year-old Marvin steered clear of them both as much as he could. Nevertheless, one hot summer night tempers flared.

In town, the family slept on cots outside under a chinaberry, or a Texas umbrella tree. Earlier that evening, Marvin had left to go swimming with Johnny Cates in a pond or irrigation ditch close by. Angie left a lamp burning for him as she bedded down for the night. She awakened much later to find the lamp still burning, and becoming fearful that Marvin had drowned, she aroused Louie and Billy to go look for him.

They hurried into their clothes. Just as Louie rounded the house, he discovered Marvin sound asleep on his cot. The boy had returned without bothering to put out the light.

This neglect provoked Louie, and he began haranguing his mother about being an alarmist. Billy called him down for talking that way to their mother. Soon there was a free-for-all between the two young men under the umbrella tree.

Marvin and Angie pulled at first one and then the other, trying to separate them. That made Louie and Billy even madder. Fearing that they might kill each other and not knowing how else to stop the fight, Angie threw herself on a cot, crying and screaming dramatically. Both boys came running to see what was wrong with their mother.

With the fight over, both young men declared that they would never again live in the same house. Angie had heard this before and talked them into going back to bed, just for the night.

When the hard breathing died down, Louie began to giggle. Billy giggled in return, and then Angie joined in. Everyone laughed as Louie came to the realization that Marvin and his mother hadn't been taking sides. They had just wanted to stop the fight. Angie observed,

**That was about the last major tussle between the boys, and I am happy to be able to say that my family is a united one.**

Angie watched her boys turn into young men with an extraordinary amount of motherly pride. In her estimation, they could do no wrong.

One evening stood out in her memory as she tried to prepare herself mentally for a town meeting about incorporation. Yes, incorporation had finally caught up with Casa Grande. But her attention went to Louie, as she watched him carefully dressing for some affair at the high school and noted how handsome he looked in his white shirt, dark trousers, and new straw hat. She must have expected the meeting to turn ugly because she remembered thinking that Louie wouldn't hesitate to swing a good right arm in her defense if the occasion should arise. She asked him to meet her after the meeting so they could walk home together. Her expectations were proved right, to a point:

**Fur did fly at the meeting, but we managed to get through it without bloodshed. The vote showed a majority in favor of town incorporation. With a sigh of relief, I looked outside for my son.**

There on the curb was the unmistakable white shirt and white straw hat. As she came out of the meeting, engaged in conversation, she felt suddenly tired. Absentmindedly, she squatted on her heels and leaned against the back of the familiar shirt while continuing to talk. "What has become of that musically gifted newcomer?" she asked Ward Davies. "I didn't see him at the meeting."

Ward smiled. "That's 'im you're leaning on."

Angie jumped up and peered into the smiling face of another young man. All the bystanders joined in for a hearty laugh at her confusion over the mistaken identity.

*SEVEN*

⁓ Misplaced Faith

WHEN ANGIE WENT TO CASA GRANDE, she believed that taking her place among the valley's peaceful settlers would be a welcome respite from the local wrangling in Wickenburg. She continued to lease the *Miner*, planning to return to Wickenburg someday, but times had changed. Like all the editors and publishers who controlled the public's only source of information, Angie had helped guide Arizona's first steps into statehood. Mines and railroads had developed the state's economy and owned many of its newspapers, but Angie's papers could freely rail against the labor practices of these corporations. She had endorsed only those candidates with progressive platforms to Arizona's Constitutional Convention in 1910 and later to the state's legislature. With the rapid changes of a growing population, with the advent of Linotype and more sophisticated printing machinery, and with the right to vote and participate in the political world, Angie could never return to that idyllic life of a country editor she had once envisioned.

She plunged into Pinal County politics by promoting Frank Pinkley, the first federal curator and caretaker of the Casa Grande Ruins, to a seat in the state senate. With his election, she bragged that Pinal County had been a Republican precinct until the *Dispatch* came along to change the minds and registrations of the voting public. Woodrow Wilson occupied the White House, and with George Hunt in the state capitol, the *Dispatch* continued receiving contracts for government printing.

Seven months after the genesis of the *Dispatch*, Angie proudly announced the installation of a large press to replace the ten-by-fifteen-foot job press she had been using.

**As the town grew, so did the business of the paper, with the result that in order to print all the news, the paper had to be enlarged. Here it is with eight six-column pages.**

During territorial days, Arizona's legislature established the post of an immigration commissioner for each county to help in persuading people around the country to settle in Arizona. An immigration commissioner's job paid around six hundred dollars a year and entailed acting as almost a one-man or one-woman chamber of commerce for the whole county.

Walt Davies, as Pinal County's current commissioner, asked Angie to help him with a display of Pinal's mineral and agricultural wealth at the state fair in Phoenix. Their display of Pima cotton, developed by the U.S. Department of Agriculture Experimental Station at Sacaton, created a buzz among cotton growers and manufacturers. Angie boomed this new type of cotton above the *Dispatch*'s masthead: "Casa Grande Valley, Home of Pima Cotton."

It came as no surprise that Pinal County supervisors would appoint Angie to the post of immigration commissioner after Walt Davies retired in 1915: she was doing this job anyway in her newspaper. In addition to placing weekly advertisements of Pinal resources in the paper, she answered inquiries about job opportunities and living conditions.

In 1916, after Casa Grande's chamber of commerce and commercial clubs fell into decay, civic leaders established a board of trade. In an effort to raise money for the board's publicity needs, Angie, Gen, Veva, and Clara Myers got together to help sponsor a show at the Airdrome, the town's new open-air entertainment facility. Gen wrote a skit, "Men Wanted," which featured her and Clara as old ladies while Angie served as their maid. Clara inserted cardboard false teeth over her own to disguise her speaking voice. When she arose to sing a duet, she remembered her false teeth and said to the audience, "Will ye excuse me if I remove me false teeth?" Angie said that after the laughter subsided, Clara and Veva burst forth with a beautiful rendition of "See the Pale Moon," and the audience was shocked into deep silence.

## Bullpatch Consolidation

The town's two rival papers often good-naturedly published news of one another's families. Angie printed a short item about Ted's son, Joe Healey:

**Leave it to the youngsters to solve perplexing problems. It takes a boy to tell 'em how. This was demonstrated one day this week by Sargent Joe Healey, son of our competitor, who is here spending his vacation. Joe says the best way to solve the newspaper problem in Casa Grande is consolidation. One paper would make good, but there are other considerations. The young man says that the solution of the whole problem is to consolidate the Bulletin and the Dispatch and then use the first syllable of the Bulletin and the last syllable of the Dispatch for its new name — *Bullpatch*.**

With the *Dispatch* outperforming the *Bulletin*, the town banker may have taken to heart Joe Healey's talk of consolidation.

Angie was surprised one day with a visit from this banker. He came right out with talk of consolidating the two newspapers and told Angie that he thought the town would be better served with one good newspaper, rather than two struggling ones. Then he dropped a bombshell. Healey wanted to sell the *Bulletin*! The banker strongly advised Angie to buy out Healey and offered to provide financing and make all the arrangements. She asked the banker to give her a few days to think it over.

Intuition warned her that this proposal didn't square with what she knew of the banker, who was a good political buddy of Healey's and who had never before taken any interest in the *Dispatch*. Friends and family all warned against the merger, even pointing out that it was probably a scheme to remove her from the newspaper field. Angie wrote,

**But the argument about one good paper in town was so potent that I was quite intrigued. I held my faith that the banker was honest in his intentions.**

Once again she ignored her intuition and gave the banker the combined machinery and equipment of both printing plants as security on a note to purchase the *Bulletin*.

On March 17, 1917, a *Dispatch* headline boldly announced: "The *Dispatch* and *Bulletin* Changes Hands. Policy of Paper Unswervingly Democratic; Strongly Independent Locally." She confidently reminisced about the history of the *Dispatch* in an article to her readers:

**For more than four years I have been trying against strong odds to give Casa Grande and the valley a good newspaper. In spite of all my efforts to turn out a neat and newsy paper only a smudgy, disheartening sheet has constantly been**

the result. This was occasioned by the impossibilities of my printing plant and of my press, which was built in the dim and distant past and had seen service in many other places before the *Dispatch* fell heir to it. The rest of the equipment is on a par with the press. Most of the machinery and type taken over from the *Bulletin* office has some ancient history of its own — some of it used by the *Florence Blade-Tribune* so long ago that only the spirit of Tom Weedin himself come back to earth could give its early history. The small job press might be designated as an interesting subject for an archeologist.

Incidentally, printing six pages, one at a time, on a job press is no small undertaking. I know what it is; I have been through it.

Thank heaven that for this issue, at least, we could use our balky engine and so print our papers without the difficulty experienced by Mr. Healey when he used the same press to print the *Bulletin*. His case was different then, and his 160 odd copies kicked off by foot power was nothing near the problem of the present *Dispatch* list.

Thank heaven again — the trials and tribulations of the *Dispatch* and the *Bulletin* are ending.

And while we are on the subject, and the reminiscent mood still persists, four years ago last September the *Bulletin* was started. Since then much has happened in our newspaper world; the *Bulletin* came and went, absorbed by the larger and stronger *Dispatch*.

When the *Bulletin* first saw the light of day it was financed absolutely by myself. This venture proved disastrous, and then for two years I labored incessantly to get out from under the load of accumulated *Bulletin* debts.

I have continued with varying success and am rather proud of my achievement. Now another page is turned, and so the future of the beloved paper is assured.

Immediately after Angie bought the *Bulletin*, an economic downturn hit all quarters of the economy as the nation prepared for war with Germany. Subscriptions went unpaid; advertising and custom printing jobs couldn't be given away. Waves of disgruntled settlers abandoned their homesteads after giving up all hope of water. Many had come on a shoestring and couldn't afford the high cost of wells and pumping. Some tried ranching, but 160 acres was sufficient to support only a few cows, not enough to make a living. For these homesteaders, the Valley of the Casa Grande didn't live up to its promises. Angie published notices of these land relinquishments with a heavy heart and began thinking that her "prophets of doom," as she called them, knew what they were talking about.

### The Secret Plan

Someone new appeared in Casa Grande looking for cheap land relinquishments and investments. Dr. MacRae had money and a yearning to write, and he hoped to get into the newspaper field. He carried camping equipment and slept in the open rather than registering in a hotel, and he would not allow his name to appear in the *Dispatch and Bulletin*. Angie often entertained him with hot biscuits and newspaper talk.

When Dr. MacRae's business associates, Mr. and Mrs. Jim Stewart, arrived in Casa Grande, Angie let them pitch a tent next to the Tin Can Mansion. Jimmie Stewart began hunting and trapping, while his wife made an analysis of the *Dispatch* ledgers and inventory.

One early morning, Jimmie excitedly awakened the Hammer family to come and see what he had trapped down by Tenney's Pond. Jimmie, being new to the West, didn't realize that, instead of a coyote, he had trapped and killed Mr. Fricke's dog.

Mrs. Stewart returned her report to Dr. MacRae. The *Dispatch* was almost as dead as Mr. Fricke's dog and didn't warrant MacRae's investment.

By this time, Angie and MacRae had exchanged confidences. He told Angie he was dodging a divorce summons, and she told him all about the water disputes, her partnership with Ted Healey, the vandalism of the printing plant, the merger of the two papers, and how she was falling behind on payments to the banker. MacRae immediately decided there was a conspiracy afoot to kill the *Dispatch* and began writing a serial called "The Secret Plan." Hoping that MacRae would change his mind and buy the *Dispatch* when he saw his story in print, Angie published his serial.

"The Secret Plan," written as a series of rather pompous morality stories told to an audience of children, contained ill-disguised allusions to real people in town. There was "The Legend of the Usurious Money Lender"; "The Legend of the Ambitions of the Poor Dupe"; "The Legend of the Town Treasury"; and so forth. The series chronicled the adventures of Stalwart Souls and Lesser Souls "who had their being in a very tiny village far, far, far away."

Casa Grande Valley, Home of Pima Cotton.   Awarded First Prize at Arizona State Fair Nov. 14, 1917, for Best Bale Long Staple Egyptian Cotton

# The Casa Grande Valley Dispatch

## And The Bulletin

Volume Six—Number Forty-Nine                    Casa Grande, Pinal County, Friday, December 21, 1917

## Judge J. E. O'Connor Is Called By Death

Former Judge James E. O'Connor passed away at Florence Saturday after a long illness due to heart trouble and other complications. Judge O'Connor has long been one of the foremost characters of this county, being active in its political, social and business life.

James Edward O'Connor was born in San Mateo county, California, February 20, 1865. His parents, James and Ellen Heffron O'Connor, were pioneers of California, having reached that state in the early fifties. Judge O'Connor's early education was acquired by study while working as a tanner and at the Oak Mound academy at Napa, California. He taught in the Napa public schools from 1889 to 1893, inclusive, studying law when he had time. He was admitted to the bar in 1892, and thereafter practiced at Napa, Madera and San Jose.

## THAT SECRET PLAN!

### WITH A CLIMAX AND A MORAL

CHAPTER TWO

[Being a continuation of the simple chronicles of Four Stalwart Souls and some Lesser, yea, verily, Much Lesser Souls who lived and had their being in ye long, long ago in a very tiny village far, far, far away.]

Now, children, gather close around and listen very carefully, and if you are very good, very very good children, you may, perhaps, learn yet a little more of that FAMOUS Secret Plan everybody is whispering about to his neighbor; but first I must tell you that there is so very, very much to tell you that you must be extremely patient children and abide the time and the hour—for of all the warmth that goeth before nothing can in anywise compare with the Climax and with the Moral—especially the Moral—so now sit quite still, children, quite still, and do not wiggle,

oh, well beloved, and we shall ascend by slow and easy grades, using words of only one syllable to meet your infantile understanding, up, up, up to the scintillating Climax—and to the Moral. Best of all, oh, well beloved, is the Moral. Now do not forget.

Now let's see, children; where were we? Do I hear someone say "axe" and "freshly ground" and "bearing aloft!" Yes, even so, children; now I remember "bearing aloft a freshly ground axe," and so let's begin just about there. Now, of course it really is not quite fair to you children to keep you in even the least suspense except in the interest of the story; not quite fair, that is, but necessary, for 'twould never, never, never do, dear ones, to spill the beans, as it were, prematurely, now would it? Of course not, but just be stupidly

long, long ago, there are a number of things, quite a number of things, children, which first you must know and understand in order, of course, that you may the better know and the more fully understand that which is coming—that Climax and that Moral. Don't forget that Moral, dear ones.

You know, oh happy, sweet, contented listeners, that all this series of tales and of the legends which must naturally and obviously accompany and elucidate this spiritual story of ye long, long ago and of the happenings in that tiny ancient village, that all this material came down to us and has been laboriously translated from a huge volume of papyrus found with many small bundles of separate sheets all deep in excavations many, many cubits beneath the surface and quite out of sight—oh, quite,

## Cotton Growers' Assn. Secretary Visits Valley

W. H. Knox, secretary and manager of the Arizona Cotton Growers' Association, spent Thursday in town in the interest of the organization, which promises to be of great value to the cotton industry here and has already saved the growers of the state an enormous amount of money to them last year.

The association is reorganized along more satisfactory lines than formerly, and instead of charging a certain fee in advance regardless of production there will be a charge of $2.00 per bale which is found to work much better.

Mr. Knox estimates there will be more than 136,000 acres of cotton planted the coming season, of which about 15,000 acres will be in Casa Grande district. Those interested in a local branch of the state organization should get in touch with Mr. Knox at once.

In connection with the matter

The name *Bulletin* was added to the *Dispatch* masthead after Angie bought out her competitor in 1917.

It may have been the story about the "Usurious Money Lender" or it may have been an item in the newspaper about some unnamed individual's interest in buying the *Dispatch* that raised consternation with the bank's board of directors. After missing payments on her note, Angie was summoned before this board of directors to show cause. She wrote,

**Apparently, The Secret Plan did worry my mortgagors. I can see them yet, looking like ogres about to devour me. If I didn't have the money, why didn't I borrow from my relatives or do this or that? The banker gave me a ten-day notice before putting my plant up for sale.**

She frantically tried to incorporate the *Dispatch* within that ten-day time limit.

**But before I could get a good start, ten days had elapsed and my chief high executioner appeared with officers of the law. One by one, different pieces of machinery were sold or moved to a nearby place with my erstwhile partner in charge.**

Gone were the Country Campbell Press, cases of type, the Washington Press, and the job press. Nothing existed in the *Dispatch* plant but one single office chair.

The banker found Angie sitting on this chair, a tired and despondent woman, approaching her midyears. He patted her graying head in a fatherly manner but couldn't disguise the smirk in his voice. "There, there, don't take it so hard, Mrs. Hammer. You'll soon see that it's for the best. Women just aren't cut out for newspaper work."

Angie's eyes flashed. "No! You're very wrong, Mr. C.! You've overlooked one thing that wasn't included in the mortgage." She pulled the *Dispatch*'s subscription list from her apron pocket and waved it in the air. "This is the soul of the *Dispatch*, and I intend to keep it."

The banker lashed out. "You must be crazy to think you can get away with this!" With that, he stalked out of the office grinding his cigar between clenched teeth, stood on the sidewalk a few moments, then came back and addressed Angie in a more conciliatory tone. "How much will you take for that list?"

"Two thousand dollars cash and no less!" She hesitated. "On second thought, the subscription list isn't for sale at any price!"

"Now I know you're crazy! You're done for in this town! I'll see to it that you never set foot in the newspaper business again!"

The *Bulletin* gleefully resumed publication while Angie scraped up enough money to have her paper printed in Phoenix. However, she couldn't continue having the paper printed out of town without losing the government contract, which stipulated that announcements be printed locally. From the *Chandler Arizonan*, she bought a well-worn six-column Diamond Press that she said was the most obstreperous piece of machinery ever invented.

Those associated with the *Bulletin* operation watched the delivery of this relic, wondering at her audacity. Didn't she know when to give up?

For the most part, her advertisers and subscribers remained true to the *Dispatch* while she cobbled together a makeshift printing plant. A. C. Taylor Printing in Phoenix extended credit for used type, but there was a serious shortage of capital letters, which required switching type from one job to the next. Louie sharpened a column rule on one side and cut notches in it to make the perforations on carbon business forms, and the boys put together a makeup table with a galvanized iron top.

A ray of sunshine broke through the clouds with an order to print the *Cotton City News*, a promotion sheet for the new town of Eloy. By this time, the United States had entered the war in Europe, but even war news held little interest to local readers. The *Dispatch* limped on with its meager supply of type.

## Prodding with a Sharp Stick

The genesis of the Reclamation Service began with Theodore Roosevelt, who promoted the reclaiming of arid federal lands in the West through the use of water development projects. Beneficiaries of these water projects had to repay the government but didn't pay interest and were allowed subsidized hydroelectricity. In 1901, California was granted its first big diversion project to supply Colorado River water to the Imperial Valley.

Arizona submitted requests to the Reclamation Service for projects on the Gila and Salt Rivers. Much of the land along the Salt River was owned by private speculators and corporations with clout in Washington, while the proposed irrigation district for Casa Grande and Florence contained the Gila River Indian Reservation. It came as no surprise that the Reclamation Service chose to build Roosevelt Dam on the Salt River in 1910. After having spent so much money for this project, Congress wanted to do nothing more for a region with sparse population and little political clout.

The peaceful Pima and Maricopa Indians had long irrigated their crops of wheat, corn, melons, squash, and cotton with water from the Gila River. Not only were these industrious people self-sustaining, they had supplied early pioneers with their produce and the Hayden Flour Mill in Tempe with wheat. But with the water above their Gila River Reservation diverted by the brush dams and canals of settlers, they received less and less water until they could no longer farm and became impoverished wards of the federal government.

Congress couldn't continue to ignore the Indians' pleas for water even though the Reclamation Service's engineers had reported earlier that there were no feasible dam sites on the Gila River for storing water. Instead, nine deep wells were drilled on the reservation and were optimistically termed the San Tan Irrigation Project. While the Indians maintained that the brackish, alkaline water from these wells was not fit for irrigation, an engineer for the Indian Agency claimed that the quality of water in these wells could not be improved upon.

Angie noted,

**The Indian Rights Association in Washington sent a female attorney, Helen Gray, to investigate the situation. She unearthed plenty in the way of schemes of land sharks to monopolize the water of the Gila River and foist the brackish well water off on the Indians.**

The mastermind of this San Tan Irrigation Project was an irrigation engineer for the Bureau of Indian Affairs by the name of William Code, who also happened to be the vice president of Dr. A. J. Chandler's bank in Mesa. The drilling of these wells was a deliberate attempt to saddle the Indians with such a large debt that they would be forced to relinquish 180,000 acres to Dr. Chandler, via the government, and relocate 90 percent of their population to San Tan. When a clerk in the Sacaton Indian Agency blew the whistle on this scheme, it made Congress markedly more sympathetic toward the Indians but highly suspicious of other proposed projects involving the Gila River.

Angie editorialized about other underhanded dealings, such as the Sligh-Fennemore scheme. In this, a group of large landholders came together under the banner of the "San Carlos Land Owners" to prevent settlers and Indians from receiving water from the Florence Canal Company. Angie said this group of farmers sincerely believed there was not enough water to go around.

Angie didn't back down on her stand against the pumping of groundwater and continually exhorted *Dispatch* readers to support the Casa Grande Water Users in their effort to build a gravity irrigation project by means of a Florence–Casa Grande Canal. Her concern lay mainly in the future of the valley. Thus, her stand against pumping underwent constant criticism from the *Bulletin* and opponents who claimed that government irrigation projects, such as the proposed San Carlos Dam, would take too long to complete. Angie defended her position:

> If it should so happen that the pumping propositions, as a means of further reclamation of the valley should be attacked, the *Dispatch* would have just as much to say in behalf of pumping. No one is pointing to the few dry holes so far encountered to prove that pumping will be a failure. In one place a dry hole may be encountered, and at another point twenty feet away, a well may be brought in. However there is really no comparison between the pumping plants of the valley and such projects as the San Carlos or Water Users Association in which hundreds of people are vitally interested, while pumping in its present stage concerns the individual only.

Because of the plight of the Indians, Congress finally authorized the funds for the Army Corps of Engineers to conduct an overall feasibility study of a storage dam at the San Carlos Reservation site above Florence. The army engineers reported favorably on the San Carlos site but recommended judicial determination of water rights before beginning construction. In February of 1914, *Dispatch* headlines jubilantly announced this favorable report, and valley residents held a big celebration at the Airdrome, a bit premature, perhaps, in light of the years of litigation and congressional wrangling that was yet to come.

Western water law revolved around the concept of prior appropriation: "first in time, first in use." Obviously, the Indians had used the Gila water since antiquity, so Representative Carl Hayden assured Congress that the Indians would have priority water rights, but he also urged the idea of a joint-use system with water to be shared equally between Indians and non-Indians. Congress wanted this project constructed and administered by the Bureau of

Indian Affairs, a change of position that didn't sit well with white landowners. It took two years for Judge A. C. Lockwood of Cochise County to halfway settle the non-Indian claims to the Gila River water. Angie was in the position of promoting Pinal County's agricultural development while discouraged settlers moved out of the valley, Indians cried for water, and Congress's attention became diverted to the war.

Huge storms caused even more destruction on the reservation. Reverend Dirk Lay, a Presbyterian minister at Sacaton Reservation on the Gila River Reservation, and the National Federation of Women's Clubs spearheaded a massive letter-writing campaign to Congress pleading the Indian's cause. As a result, Congress paid more attention to Representative Hayden's proposal to fund two diversion dams on the reservation as the initial step in a joint-use irrigation system. This way, some of the cost could be borne by private landowners, instead of the government footing the entire bill.

In 1916, after the Army Corps of Engineers gave the green light for building these diversion dams, and Judge Lockwood finalized the adjudication of water rights, Congress appropriated money to begin construction. Nothing happened. Valley residents waited and waited.

Angie finally took matters into her own hands and wrote to Senator Ashurst to see why the project was being held back. He responded in a letter dated October 8, 1917.

Dear Mrs. Hammer,

This is in reply to yours of the third, and [I] am not surprised over your anxiety, for I, myself, am very much nettled and almost angry over the apparent endless delay in the Department respecting the construction of the diversion dam above Florence. I have prodded the Honorable Secretary of the Interior and the Commissioner of Indian Affairs with a sharp stick several times on this subject, and shall certainly lay this matter before Secretary Lane personally as soon as he returns.

Immediately upon acquiring any information with respect to the present status and contemplated action in the matter, I will advise you.

Henry F. Ashurst

Senator Ashurst took Angie's letter to the Department of the Interior and received this reply from the acting secretary of the Committee on Indian Affairs on October 19, 1917. Since the Indians weren't allowed to speak for themselves, the secretary of the Interior Department was their spokesman.

> My Dear Senator:
>
> On October 10th, you called upon me with reference to the construction of the proposed diversion dam on the Gila River and left with me a letter from Mrs. Angela H. Hammer, editor and proprietor of the *Casa Grande Valley Dispatch*, concerning the matter.
>
> It appears that Mrs. Hammer has been misinformed as to the situation. The act authorizing this project provides that it shall only be undertaken if the Secretary of the Interior shall be able to make or provide for what he deems to be satisfactory adjustments of the rights to the water to be diverted by said diversion dam or carried in canals, and satisfactory arrangements for the inclusion of lands within said project and the purchase of property rights which he shall deem necessary to be acquired, and shall determine and declare the said project to be feasible.
>
> With a view to making such an adjustment of the rights to the water to be diverted as would enable the department to comply with the terms of the act, there was prepared a form of contract to be executed by the respective claimants. This form was approved May 16th, and it has since been in the hands of the persons representing the Water Users, but no indication has been received as to whether it will be acceptable to the parties concerned, and if not, to give them the opportunity to suggest desirable changes.
>
> It occurs to me that if Mrs. Hammer would care to publish the form in her paper, that might be an excellent way of putting it before the public. Therefore, I am enclosing a copy of it which, if you deem advisable, you may send her.
>
> Alexander T. Vogelsang

Angie was shocked to discover that it was the water users association, not the government agencies, that had caused the long delay. Construction on the diversion dams couldn't begin until a Landowners' Agreement was signed. In this agreement all non-Indians had to assign their land and "inchoate," or newly acquired, water rights over to the Department of the Interior as collateral for government funding.

The old Casa Grande Water Users Association headed by John Fred Brown had gone bankrupt in their efforts to build the Casa Grande–Florence Canal. Angie wrote,

**They had elected a new board of directors. This new board had either missed the significance of the government letter and its accompanying forms, or it was buried under a load of mail.**

In what Angie considered the *Dispatch*'s finest hour, she sounded the alarm for landowners and homestead entrymen to join the new water users group and sign the required contracts. Many were still skeptical of a project being administered by the Indian Service, but the *Dispatch* trumpeted the Landowners' Agreement as a great victory for the water users association.

However, it was a headline story about a cold-blooded murder, not water politics, that captured the attention of Casa Grande residents. Waves of shock reverberated throughout Pinal County.

### Dad Tenney's Murder

Old man Cummings saw the whole thing from the upper deck of his two-story apartment. He heard the single shot and saw Dad Tenney, the town's only police officer, rush into one of the adobe houses to investigate. Jesus Muñoz had just shot his common-law wife. Another shot rang out, and Dad staggered to the street and fell. Muñoz followed him out, stooped down to take Dad's gun and cartridge belt, fired two more rounds into the officer's head, and fled down the railroad tracks. Old man Cummings, as crippled as he was, hobbled down the stairs with his gun, vowing to avenge the death.

The most coherent story Angie could get came from Herman Veith, who owned the ice cream parlor next to the McKinley Restaurant. He said a crowd assembled out of nowhere, all heavily armed. Herman joined this crowd, which followed Muñoz down the railroad tracks to a pile of boulders. A shot whizzed past Herman's head, missing him by a few inches. He turned to see old man Cummings blazing his way toward the murderer.

Judge Charles F. Bennett, justice of the peace, hobbled behind the crowd with the aid of his cane. By the time he came to the boulders, Muñoz had used up all his ammunition and was found slumped over, dead. Judge Bennett ordered the body removed from the rocks and empanelled a coroner's jury. After inspecting the eighty-some bullet holes in the body, the jury decided that Muñoz came to his death from gunshots fired by persons unknown. The murder of Casa Grande's beloved lawman had been avenged by practically the whole town.

A *Dispatch* article about the murder, dated April 6, 1918, credited Sheriff Rye Miles of Pima County, who happened to be in town at the time, with killing the crazed Muñoz. Angie didn't authorize this story because she no longer published the *Dispatch*. Her farewell to Casa Grande readers explained why.

**After five years of effort, in behalf of the Valley and County, I have severed my connections with the *Casa Grande Valley Dispatch*. Mr. I. T. Holland, who has been identified with the paper for the past few months, is now its business manager. In turning the paper over to its new owners, it is with the feeling that it is in good hands.**

**It is with a certain degree of regret that I quit the weekly talks and close contact with the *Dispatch* family of subscribers, but I hand over the reins with the hope of serving them and all the people of the County and State in another way, by becoming their representative in the State Legislature.**

**"Our First Duty is to Win the War." This is the slogan of the Hammer family. To that end, my two elder sons have volunteered their services to the nation, and to the same end, all the strength and influence I may be able to exert in the legislature will be directed if the voters of the county see fit to honor me with the nomination for the office I seek.**

**As to the *Dispatch*, I bespeak for it the continued generous patronage of the business people of Casa Grande and a real live interest in its affairs by its subscribers.**

# *EIGHT*

## ∼ Fissionable Thought

THE ARMY BEGAN DRAFTING twenty-one-year-olds. Since Louie and his mechanic buddy, Blinky Wilson, were both twenty-one, they enlisted in the Thirty-sixth Division's Mobile Ordnance Unit to serve as automotive mechanics and truck drivers. Billy signed up a short time later. The Casa Grande Women's Club raised money and presented each young man with a wristwatch before he was sent away for induction.

The troop train transporting Louie and Blinky east to Fort Bliss rolled into Casa Grande. Across the face of the depot a banner read, "Farewell and Good Luck to Blinky and Louie, Our Hometown Heroes." As the locomotive pulled up to the water tank, Angie strained for a first, and maybe last, glimpse of her son before he left for France.

Louie's pal, Blinky, resplendent in a new army uniform, appeared in the caboose, waving and blowing kisses to the well-wishers. Angie inched her way forward. "Blinky, where's Louie?" she called. "Is he sick?"

Her voice was drowned out by Casa Grande's band playing the final refrains of *Over There*. Blinky didn't see or hear her. The train lurched forward in a cloud of steam, leaving a distraught mother close to panic.

Woman suffrage had come to Arizona along with statehood in 1912, but in 1918, when Angie tossed her bonnet into Pinal's legislative race, it would be another two years before women in the United States gained the constitutional right to vote. In Arizona, a few of Angie's contemporaries had become active in the political arena, but a lot of skepticism about women's roles still remained in the minds of voters. Between campaign speeches in Florence and Casa Grande,

Angie knitted sponges and made gauze bandages and muslin slings for the Red Cross. She spent her nights praying.

Angie traced her defeat in the legislative race back to a caustic article she'd written about a special water users' meeting in Florence. She wrote that she lost her bid by a small margin of votes—not enough to feel that nobody loved her.

Mrs. Frank Plotts, president of the local Red Cross chapter, sent out an S.O.S. for money to buy supplies. Just as they always did, the Casa Grande Women's Club stepped up to plan a fund-raising event, a street fair that would include every social club and business in town. Angie's favorite banker told Mrs. Plotts the idea was crazy: the street fair would cost more to stage than the Red Cross could possibly gain. That, of course, was all Angie needed to hear. These women would prove that a single-minded group of women could accomplish the impossible. Instead of spending money to build booths, the women brought old blankets and draperies from home.

A parade of floats kicked off the street fair. The Red Cross float depicted a realistic tableau of a nurse and doctor tending a wounded soldier. Another float featured a wagonload of children dressed to look like flowers and touted as the "Finest Products of the Casa Grande Valley." Everyone caught some kind of prize in a fishpond under the town water tank.

Angie visited a fortune-telling booth at the fair. After gazing into her crystal ball, the fortune-teller said, "I see that one of your sons will not come back from the war."

Bolting out of the booth, Angie yelled back, "Don't you dare put that thought out into the universe."

The Red Cross bought three hundred dollars' worth of gauze and muslin with the money they made at the fair, and Angie repressed a desire to tell the banker, "I told you so."

A letter arrived from France, where Louie repaired weapons and vehicles near the front. He hoped his mother hadn't been too upset when he didn't appear at Casa Grande's send-off. It was all Blinky's fault, he wrote. He had been sleeping off the effects of diphtheria, smallpox, and malaria shots and had asked Blinky to awaken him before the train arrived at Casa Grande. Blinky thought it was a huge joke to let Louie sleep through the town's farewell.

Louie went on to write about the effects of hunger, nerve gas, trench mouth, and influenza upon troops waiting in trenches for supplies that never came. He'd seen starving American soldiers cross the "no man's land" between the front lines to get into French beet fields, only to be shot by hidden Germans.

He also wrote about the wonder of airplanes, both German and American, which photographed enemy movements from above. Once an airplane with an American insignia flew low over his trench. The pilot shouted that he'd return with a food drop. Sensing something wrong, they abandoned the trench and watched as this airplane returned to drop bombs, not food.

Meanwhile, the military's need for long-staple cotton used in the manufacture of airplane wings and tires sent the demand for this product spiraling. Deep tube wells probed underground for more water to irrigate thousands of newly planted acres of the "white gold." Angie's job as immigration commissioner took on hectic proportions as she answered inquiries about available land and living conditions in the county. The value of land increased to such an extent that J. F. Brown sold his 320-acre ranch for 45,000 dollars and took off to serve Allied telegraphy needs in Europe. But this sudden prosperity couldn't keep the Spanish influenza bug, which had taken the lives of so many servicemen and people in the East, from making its way into Arizona.

### Dr. Gungle's Triple X

One of the town's first flu victims was Maizie Fordham. Dr. Gungle and Angie rushed to her bedside in the Palms Hotel, where Dr. Gungle prescribed his Triple X medicine and directed Angie to apply hot towels and Vick's Vapo-Rub to Maizie's chest and throat to keep her air passages open. Angie was also instructed to disinfect all the rooms and furnishings in the hotel with formaldehyde.

When Maizie began to recover, Dr. Gungle sent Angie directly to the Charles French home, where Mrs. French battled the flu. By this time, nurses were in short supply because almost everyone in town was either sick or taking care of someone else. Mrs. French felt she needed fresh air and sunshine, so she went for a walk, soon tired, and sat upon the ground to rest. This effort supposedly caused her to relapse into a virulent form of the flu that caused hemorrhaging from the lungs. Angie lost her second patient within three days, but before she could rest, Dr. Gungle asked her to go to the aid of a pregnant woman in Sacaton who would surely die without immediate care.

She attended the pregnant woman day and night for a week, and the patient recovered. On her way home from Sacaton, Angie suffered the telltale flu symptoms: nausea, chills, and fever. She went to bed in the Tin Can Mansion with Marvin as her nurse.

While resting in bed, Angie idly flipped through her boys' *Popular Science* magazines and happened across an article that was to become an epiphany. The article described an experiment where participants propelled a tiny disk balanced on a needle to any point on a smooth surface, either fast or slow, by the power of their minds alone. This article concluded that human thought must be an electrical force of some kind. Elated by what she considered definitive proof of something she had always suspected, she later wrote in her memoirs:

> **I reasoned that if an inanimate thing like that gadget could be moved by thought, I could see where such a force directed at conditions and people could be effective. We know by observation that thoughts can be sparked and flashed from one person to another to create good or bad in the world. I began to conceive of brainpower as fissionable, capable of setting off mental atomic bombs. [Note: This was written after World War II.]**

She immediately contacted Pattie, Addie, and Monica to tell them of her discovery. The notion came as no news to Monica, already a Christian Scientist who believed in the power of prayer to bring about healing. Long before Sarah's death, Angie and her sisters had begun searching for a philosophy to replace Catholic doctrine, a quest that possibly led to further estrangement from their mother. These rather intellectual women could no longer accept the tenet of infants being born in sin. Angie, in particular, believed that it was circumstances of birth and conditions in society that lead people astray, not sin. The women delved into books and held great debates over the hot topics of the day—including hypnotism and mind over matter.

They all became followers of Ernest Holmes and listened to his weekly radio program, "This Thing Called Life." Holmes claimed, "There is a power for good in the Universe and you can use it." The power Holmes talked about, both individual and collective thought, created the conditions of external reality.

When Marvin came down with the flu, Angie had time to reflect on Dr. Holmes' philosophy. Undoubtedly, words as a medium of thought conveyed powerful suggestions to the public consciousness. She began examining her own writing in light of this revelation.

> **Every time I wrote an editorial when I was upset, it was met with adverse reactions. Whenever I wrote from a positive standpoint, a warm, comfortable**

**glow enfolded me, and there was sure to be nice comments on what I had written.**

Even after Marvin's recovery, Dr. Gungle wasn't through with Angie and the flu scourge. He summoned her to the aid of a rancher who died shortly after she arrived. Then the rancher's wife became ill, and Angie stayed awake on black coffee for over a week while ministering to her. When Dr. Gungle came to check the patient, he told Angie to go home. "The patient is in better shape than you are." She slept for three days, straight through the celebration that marked the ending of World War I.

Louie, Billy, and Blinky returned home, confounding the fortune-teller. Louie brought his mother the standard war trophies, a German helmet with spiked cross and copper shell casings made into brass vases, and then retired to a cot under the umbrella tree, where he lay depressed and uncommunicative for a month. Angie claimed that her son's ideals, if not his nerves, had been shattered in the war.

Eventually, Louie went to work in the copper mines at Ray, Arizona, pulling together his mind and body through hard labor.


### To Sell a Dead Horse

The *Dispatch* had changed hands several times in the two years since Angie had sold it. Operating on a slim-to-nonexistent profit margin, each new owner fought to keep the worn-out, labor-intensive machinery in operation, which couldn't be done. The current owner, Mr. M. A. Davis, told Angie he would abandon the *Dispatch* if she didn't take it back. He couldn't continue making payments on a dead horse.

Angie hesitated, but she didn't want to see her beloved paper die. It was a tough decision because, for the first time in her life, she was making a comfortable living.

When her friend, Clara Myers, had been about to lose her landholdings for back taxes, she had asked Angie's help in selling her lots. Angie designed promotional leaflets and ads. Some of the valley's big cotton farmers were German Lutheran, so she went to their church to distribute the leaflets and talk to them about building homes in town. In five days, she had sold eighty-five of Clara's lots for cash.

Angie took her usual courtesy poll of family and friends about reviving the

*Dispatch.* Everyone voiced opposition. The general theme was, How could she even consider taking back the paper after the hardships she had endured? Louie argued vehemently, telling his mother to sell the paper for anything she could get.

Upon hearing this, Angie made a snap decision. "A dead horse is not salable for anything but fertilizer. I'm going to revive the *Dispatch* and use my commission from lot sales to clear the plant of debt."

In November of 1919, the *Dispatch* resumed business. Angie renewed credits for many of her former subscribers and fell back on her expertise in advertising design. Merchants had only to tell her verbally what they wanted their ad to say. She would then write up the copy, design the layout, and set the type herself, thereby saving the merchants a lot of time and trouble.

Angie began needling the opposition with little short squibs, some factual and some imaginary, about people looking over the banking field in Casa Grande. As Mark Twain used to say, "I just invent the news whenever reality lets me down." Angie further embroidered the news by writing that the proposed new concern would be named the First National Bank of Casa Grande.

This fabrication caught the attention of a group of local businessmen, who may have been planning to open a bank anyway. Within a few months, the First National Bank of Casa Grande opened its doors with George Lavers as president and John Fred Brown as a member of the board. Albert Marion Peck, soon to be Louie's father-in-law, was the bank's cashier. When the bank opened its doors for business, Angie was first in line with a large deposit for printing high-paying mining claim patent notices. She talked to George Lavers about a loan for new machinery, maybe even one of the Linotype machines that all the big newspapers had begun to use to eliminate the need for setting type by hand. Mr. Lavers agreed to help her.

A short time later, Will C. Fischer, a salesman for the American Type Founders, dropped by the *Dispatch* office. Angie inquired about the cost of a used Merganthaler Linotype.

"Why sure, we have one on the floor right now. It's a Model Five that I can get for you on easy terms—just what you need here."

True to his word, George Lavers and the First National Bank of Casa Grande handled the Linotype loan that cost Angie fifty dollars a month.

According to the grapevine, the *Bulletin* camp watched the delivery of Angie's Merganthaler with glee, saying that now Angie would go broke in

The Casa Grande Battery Company, Louie Hammer and Bud Bottriell's first garage, on West Second Street in Casa Grande.

short order. She was in way over her head because she wouldn't be able to keep the Linotype running without constantly calling in machinists from out of town.

What the opposition didn't understand was that Angie already had the best machinist in the country. After an installing engineer briefed Marvin on the operation of the Merganthaler, and he conquered an initial problem with the lead melting pot that operated by means of a gasoline burner, Angie had no need to call in machinists.

The *Dispatch* emerged as a modern, full-fledged newspaper with such features as agricultural news, California house plans, and the current technology of crystal radios and automotive repair and maintenance. Even the most trivial items, a resident's trip to Phoenix or Mrs. Peart's purchase of baby chicks, made their way into the *Dispatch* columns. Folks loved to see their names in print, and names sold newspapers.

As the great "noble experiment" brought Prohibition to the nation, the alcohol consumption of Angie's printers increased. She said they developed expertise in sniffing out all the "blind pigs," or illegal stills in the countryside. If they couldn't find "white mule," they resorted to flavoring extract, Jamaican ginger, or any other concoction that had a kick. But it wasn't just the printers that made Angie regret her former stand as a White Ribboner; the illegal liquor industry brought with it a new social order with all its accouterments of intrigue and danger. Angie editorialized:

**Even some of the high school kids are bootlegging and bringing their wares to dances. In former times, a girl wouldn't dance with a boy who had the odor of liquor about him, so it is a shocking denouement to find that women's garment manufacturers make skirts with flask pockets so girls can carry their own booze.**

Louie returned from the mines in Ray. He and his partner, Maurice "Bud" Bottriell, purchased a battery shop that in later years became an automotive garage.

## A Blast of Tobacco Juice

Town characters provided comic relief from the more serious side of newspaper work and occasionally made the columns of the *Dispatch*. In her memoirs, Angie fondly described Windy Bill and his dog Speedy, writing that Windy's old, crumpled felt hat covered long, stringy hair, and a slimy mustache hid his snaggly front teeth. Windy would sidle up close to people when he talked. She learned to step aside or else get sprayed with a blast of tobacco juice. Each day Windy made his rounds, stopping first at the *Dispatch* office to gab, then visiting all the babies and young mothers in town. Windy loved babies and dogs.

One day Windy barged into the *Dispatch* office, raving about his narrow escape from a disgraceful death in Phoenix the day before. "I come close to gettin' run over by a baby buggy pushed by the biggest, meanest woman you ever saw. It's bad enough to be kilt under the wheels of a powerful automobile; that could give a fellow's death a kind of dignity. But I'd be the laughingstock of the country if I bit the dust under such a puny thing as a baby buggy." Windy snorted as Angie dodged a spray of tobacco juice.

"Why, Bill, I thought you were bringing me some bit of important mining news. How about something from the Jackrabbit Mining District? You know a lot about what's going on there."

"Yes, I know plenty, but what's the use? It's all shut down and what's left ain't worth talking about. But I'll tell you what I do remember most about the Jackrabbit Mine. Me and some other fellas used to go help out the old watchman at the mine. The poor devil was all crippled up with rheumatiz. He couldn't do nuthin' but sit and watch and hobble around a little. One day the old fella up and died on us."

"What did you do then?"

"There warn't nothin' we could do but give him a decent wake. We made a wooden coffin and got the old-timer's body ready for burial. But we had a devil of a time makin' him lie down, 'cause he was so bent up from that rheumatiz that we had to tie him down. After we got him down, we put the coffin on a couple sawhorses in the company dining room and gathered for last honors to a brother miner."

"Did you have a religious service?"

"Oh, yes, sorta. We spent the evening tellin' yarns about the deceased, discussing his good points and his bad ones. In the middle of a bad one, the corpse suddenly sat bolt upright in his casket. Oh, my Gawd, was I ever scairt half to death! You should'a seen me clear that windasill and take the screen with it. The rest of the boys tore down the door gettin' out."

"How come you were afraid of a dead man, especially one so crippled up?"

"You'd a-been scairt, too, if you'd been sayin' the things we was sayin'. When we went back in to have a peek, there he was, still sittin' up in his coffin 'cause the strings we tied him down with snapped. We didn't mess around with him anymore after that. We got a coroner and let him take care of the rest of the business."

Seeing that she wasn't to get any mining news out of Windy, Angie cut him short or else he would have rambled on all day. "Bill, for the sake of your babies, hadn't you better go check on them? Their mothers might need you so they can run errands."

No one in the community would ever think of causing grief to Windy, but one day Angie saw a crowd gathering around the grizzled old man as he wildly waved a pistol at the town dogcatcher. His red bandana had worked its way around to the side of his neck. "Speedy don't need no license," Windy kept yelling. "He's a war hero dog and done more for our country than most of you good-fer-nothin' so-and-so's! You'll lock him up over my dead body."

The dogcatcher backed off. "I'm just doin' my duty, and that means impoundin' every dog not wearin' a license. Speedy needs a license just like all the rest of the dogs."

Kate Doran, a nearby restaurant owner, rushed in to speak on Speedy's behalf, while someone took the gun out of Windy's wavering hand.

Windy continued raving. "And why shouldn't I think more of this dog than any dad-blamed human on earth? He saved my life once when I was a-tryin' to crank up my old car. My hand slipped, and the crank knocked me out cold. If Speedy had'na drug me outta the hot sun, I'd a-been a goner for sure. He drug me to a wash under a highway bridge and clawed sand all over me."

After that yarn, everyone agreed that Speedy was more human than canine and didn't need a license. Even the dogcatcher agreed.

### The Clutch of Financial Disaster

The year 1920 brought financial hardships galore. The government cancelled its wartime cotton contracts, and many farmers went bankrupt. The price of copper plummeted, resulting in shutdowns of some of the county's largest mines. A continuing drought dried up springs and water tanks, leaving the desert strewn with the carcasses of dead cattle. Good times ended in Pinal County.

When the presidential primaries got under way, one of the Republican candidates, Warren Harding, proclaimed his tight-fisted budgetary intentions—a disinclination to fund Western irrigation projects. Angie editorialized vigorously against his nomination, then wrote indignantly about his selection at the Republican convention.

**Harding had already been selected in smoke-filled rooms and not by the convention delegates. If his nomination hadn't been decided in advance, why did life-sized lithographs of Harding come to blossom all over town the morning after his candidacy was announced?**

All during the presidential campaign, Angie blasted the Republicans for their slogan "Get the Money" and couldn't understand why businessmen stood by the Republican Party, regardless of how Harding's election would affect the West. She let the public know all about Harding's secretary of the interior, who became embroiled in the Elk Hill and Teapot Dome scandals and reportedly received more than four hundred thousand dollars from oil companies. Again, Angie reminded her readers of the Republican's campaign slogan.

The secretary of the interior took revenge upon Democratic newspapers all over the country when he ordered that all government printing contracts be awarded only to Republican papers. Looking back, Angie almost wished she had been a little less vocal about the election. The loss of that contract and the poor state of the economy spelled doom for the *Dispatch*. Folks lining up at soup kitchens didn't care to read the news. Merchants didn't advertise when folks had no money to buy their commodities. Angie pleaded for extensions on the Linotype note. In a letter to the Merganthaler Company on April 23, 1921, she spelled out the conditions of the valley.

**Collections for advertising, printing and subscriptions are so bad that it is nearly impossible to get in much of our money. Our cotton crop was a failure and scores of farmers are flat broke. I understand our debtors' condition. If something could be done for them, our prosperity would return.**

**However, there is one good sign. People are slipping into the valley, taking advantage of the present slump to look for land bargains. I expect to sell some of this real estate. In addition, I will put one of my sons on the linotype to dispense with an operator's salary and put the other to work on an outside job. If you grant this extension, it would make all the difference in the world to my business affairs.**

Merganthaler granted the extension, and Angie then tried to cajole her readers into making payments on their subscriptions.

**Dick Wick Hall, the editor of the *Salome Sun*, a little rag published at Salome "where she danced" is credited with having made the statement that his publication had the largest unpaid circulation of any paper in the world. We wish to take exception to that remark. While the famous dancer's press agent may be short a whole lot on subscriptions, we think the *Dispatch* holds first place at this time, but we will abdicate in favor of the *Sun* if we can.**

**Moral: If you are short of cash or inclined to be dishonest, don't let your debt to the *Dispatch* bother you, but if you are otherwise, please pay up!**

An almost fatal blow came when the landlord of the *Dispatch* building arbitrarily hiked the rent for several months in a row. Angie tried to make arrangements for partial payments until business picked up again, but the landlord refused any clemency and delivered an ultimatum. The plant would be attached if she didn't come up with all the back rent immediately.

Angie sought the help of a young attorney who had just established a practice in Casa Grande. Ernest McFarland told Angie that her tools for making a living were exempt from attachment and that the landlord should allow her to make reasonable arrangements for paying the back rent. McFarland apprised the landlord of the indefensible position he had taken with the newspaper.

Greatly impressed with this lawyer, Angie told her boys, "McFarland is a young Lincoln, and this country will hear from him in the future."

## A Convention of Foolish Mules

In May of 1922, Angie served as one of Pinal's delegates to the Democratic conference in Tucson. This committee, led by Ernest McFarland, pledged to nominate Charles B. Ward for governor, but at the last minute, the Democrats' prodigal son, George W. P. Hunt, blew into the convention and declared himself a candidate. As Arizona's first state governor, Hunt had served two terms before being selected by President Wilson as ambassador to Siam. Turmoil and dissention followed in the wake of Hunt's sudden appearance at the nominating convention.

Angie did what she could to pull the party together by printing and distributing a hastily put-together poem playing on the Democratic Party symbol. This corny attempt at unification did little good, but Angie had fun writing it.

*Will the Democrats Ever Learn?*

Two foolish mules, each filled with hope,
    Were fastened together with some rope.
Said one to the other, "Come my way,
    And watch me while I eat my hay."
They each pulled and galled their necks,
    Both were strictly on the peck.
They faced each other, those stubborn brats,
    And said, "We're like FOOL DEMOCRATS.
Pulling together is the only way,
    We can insure against loss of hay."
In conference they agreed, each with the other,
    Instead of quarrelling, they'd be like brothers.

Compliments of *Casa Grande Valley Dispatch*, 1922

With the exception of Charles B. Ward, the Pinal County committee's entire slate of candidates won the primary election. Hunt won the gubernatorial race by a good majority, but Angie said the upset of the principle of party unity was in evidence for years to come.

Governor Hunt's opponents liked to portray him as a rude, crude ignoramus, lacking in table manners and social skills. After one of his speaking engagements in Casa Grande, his presence at a local restaurant attracted a crowd of onlookers. They congregated inside the front door and around the windows. When Governor Hunt spotted some of his known antagonists watching him, he dropped his fork, put both elbows on the table, and began shoveling peas into his mouth with a knife. The governor didn't crack a smile as hilarity engulfed the assemblage.

Politicians often court the favor of newspaper editors, but in Angie's case, Governor Hunt courted her son. It all began when the governor invited Louie to join a group of young men on his road inspection tour to the Grand Canyon. Impressed with Louie's mechanical skills, intelligence, and wit, he asked the young man to chauffeur him on other trips around the state. The governor then presented Angie with a complete set of snapshots taken on their journeys. Not only did Hunt clearly hope to mentor Louie into a political career, Angie began to suspect him of an additional motive. Judging from Louie's numerous invitations to the governor's home, she wondered if Hunt was trying to match Louie with his daughter, Virginia.

The landlord tiff resulted in the *Dispatch* being moved to the Boroff Building on Florence Street in late 1922. There, Angie met a personable young woman, Jewel Winbourne Ircompte, who came seeking employment. Since Jewel had some business training in her background, Angie hired her to work in the advertising department of the paper. Jewel devoted so much time to this rough grind that she rented the upstairs in the Boroff Building. Both she and Angie used these quarters for afternoon naps, referring to it as their Lincoln Hotel. Jewel later married and became Jewel Jordan, the first woman sheriff of Maricopa County and then Arizona's state auditor for eighteen years.

The economic doldrums began to ease in 1923, and the *Dispatch* took on the appearance of prosperity. Angie wrote,

**People who wouldn't take the paper at any price a few months before are now in the mood to buy. All hopes of the *Dispatch* falling by the wayside for anyone to pick up at their leisure were dispelled.**

Governor George W. P. Hunt (left) and Louie in 1925.

Possibly because of political infighting, Angie decided to sever the *Dispatch*'s affiliation with the Democratic Party. Above the paper's masthead appeared the phrase: "Arizona's Most Progressive Weekly Newspaper: An Independent Paper Dedicated to the Interests of Casa Grande Valley." She printed a formal announcement of the paper's switch to independent status on March 1, 1923.

**We have reached the stage of development in our community where every effort should be put forth. This can only be accomplished when people and papers look to the returns of the valley, instead of the returns of the poll. We, as a community, can ill afford to let our inherent rights be crucified on the cross of partisan politics.**

### The Lewis Capers

With the revitalization of the *Dispatch*, Angie hired a hard-hitting editor in the person of W. T. Lewis. Mr. Lewis made a practice of scanning the editorial columns of other newspapers, looking for reasons to engage in wordy battles. He found such a reason when one editor objected to the policy change of the *Dispatch*. Round one of Mr. Lewis's miscellany of scathing editorials read:

> March 15, 1923. Bill Stuart, of the *Prescott Evening Courier*, is running true to form in so far as never having things right in his mind before the trigger of his pen is pulled and a volley of wasted journalistic effort has gone to the same place as the cork for a small boy's air gun. People's knowledge of the Honorable Bill Stuart acts as the string attached to that cork, consequently he never gets anywhere. The feeble efforts of that paper to get in the limelight of publicity would be laughable, were they not so pitiful. There has never been any move of any kind made, either political or otherwise, by Democrat or Republican, that the *Courier* has not found some objectionable feature in it. Stuart has ever been the type of journalist who builds his ideas from T.N.T. and then is surprised at what follows. It might enlighten Bill slightly if he would take a look at the masthead of the *Dispatch*.

When the *Bulletin* printed sarcastic comments about the *Dispatch*'s political switch, Lewis fired off round two.

> When the *Bulletin* refers to its funny page, it leaves the reader in doubt as to which page they are calling attention to. We presume though, it meant the page carrying the article where a Republican paper expressed regret that a Democratic paper had joined the Independents. That was funny!

The *Arizona Gazette* in Phoenix took a different view of the policy change and praised the paper.

> In an announcement on the first page of the *Casa Grande Valley Dispatch*, one of the most alert and readable of our contemporaries, the editor announced a change of policy. To all of us who are interested in the progress of journalism in Arizona, the development of new ideas and principles nailed to the masthead of the *Dispatch*, will be followed with new interest.

The Casa Grande Town Council asked both the *Dispatch* and the *Bulletin* to submit bids of cost per inch for printing ordinances, proclamations, and proceedings of council meetings. Angie's response to the council contained a flat-out bid of thirty cents per inch. Healey's written response contained no bid whatsoever. Instead, he bad-mouthed the *Dispatch* as being unreliable, promised to run the minutes of the council meetings free of charge, and offered to run the city legals at "the usual rate charged nations or states."

The council awarded the contract to the *Bulletin* without investigating the "rate charged nations or states." Little did they know that this rate was seventy-five cents per inch.

A furious Lewis turned his guns on the city council. Their every move brought scathing comments in the *Dispatch*. Time and again, the council ordered Lewis to appear before them to explain and defend the accusations he made in the paper, accusations that came dangerously close to libel.

Then one day, as Angie sat at the Linotype setting up items for the paper, a representative from the Merganthaler Company dropped in. He looked bewildered and said, "Why, that machine doesn't look as though it's been wrecked!"

When Angie asked what he meant, he responded, "There was an item in the *Los Angeles Times* about a vandal who broke into your plant and demolished your Linotype because of a grievance against your editor. I have the article right here." He showed it to Angie.

> March 18, 1923. The linotype of the *Casa Grande Valley Dispatch* has been wrecked. Some enemy entered the office after nightfall and fell upon the typesetting machine with a heavy hammer, smashing the matrix magazine and keyboard and doing damage that may cost $1500.00 to repair. The raid appeared to have been in pure malice, with some reference to the attitude of the weekly paper in a municipal campaign now in progress. The *Dispatch* is owned by Mrs. Angela H. Hammer, a veteran Arizona printer and newspaper publisher. It had been a staunch Democratic organ for years, but lately made announcement that its course would be changed and that politics thereafter would be subordinated. There was employed as editor, W. T. Lewis, formerly of Phoenix and Tucson, who permitted the publication of a number of articles sharply criticizing the city administration. The town has a second weekly, the *Bulletin*, edited by Ted Healey, a Republican.

Angie couldn't begin to make sense of this article. Surely, she thought, Mr. Lewis wouldn't write an out-and-out lie. She had stretched the truth when she wrote about a new bank coming to town, but what motive would lead Mr. Lewis to deliberately fabricate such a story?

She contacted Colonel J. H. McClintock, Arizona's correspondent for the

*Los Angeles Times*, and found him to be just as puzzled as she was. "Lewis himself handed me that story about the Linotype," he told her. "I gave it to my editor in good faith. I suspect Lewis either wants to put the city administration in a bad light or just get his name in the paper. I'll write a retraction and give it to my editor."

Lewis went berserk when Angie confronted him about the story. He raved that she and McClintock were out to get him. He vowed that he would hire a lawyer and bring a libel lawsuit against her.

When Angie told McClintock about Lewis's threat of a lawsuit, McClintock replied, "That man is deranged. He wrote a letter to my editor accusing me of trying to frame him. If he does bring charges against you, my boss says to tell you that, if necessary, he'll come to your defense in court. We have a statement signed by four different people attesting to the fact that the story about the damaged Linotype was told to them by Mr. Lewis at different times and places."

Sure enough, a letter from Lewis's lawyer notified Angie of the pending lawsuit. She told about Lewis's grievance on the front page of the *Dispatch* on March 22, 1923.

**Mr. Lewis stated in his complaint that he had become famous over the state for his progressive editorials and that if he were not permitted to continue said editorials, his standing as a high class newspaperman would be injured. Attorney Brewton A. Hayne represented Mr. Lewis and drew up a soul-stirring complaint, reciting how Mrs. Hammer pleaded with his client to save the paper from bankruptcy.**

Lewis dropped his suit against Angie and, leaving behind a trail of lies and debt, vacated Casa Grande.

Angie's days of wearing the various hats of editor, reporter, journalist, janitor, and even printer had long become a thing of the past. She replaced Mr. Lewis with Harold Henry as the next editor. He brought a whole change of climate and new readership to the *Dispatch* with his touches of levity. Here is an example of one of his irreverent columns called "Forty-eight Years Ago in Casa Grande" from November 1, 1923:

- A Sears and Roebuck catalogue has been added to the new library located next to the Damfino Saloon.

- There have been no holdups between here and Yuma for more than a week, which makes social life rather dull these days.
- The Lost Sole Dance Hall will be closed Monday while the bullet holes in the walls will be filled with adobe mud.
- A tenderfoot accidentally stepped on the foot of Wildhorse Pete in the Damfino Saloon last evening. The funeral was well attended this morning.
- A scandal broke out among the businessmen last Tuesday when the corpse spilled out of the hearse en route to the cemetery. The lid of the casket came off, exposing a cotton shroud on the corpse, instead of the pure silk material that was ordered. Since then, the other thirteen undertakers here in town have put heavy padlocks on their hearses and extra precautions have been taken in securing casket lids.
- Pima Baxter, the squaw man from Sacaton, bet his wife against five dollars in a poker game at the Desert Rat Saloon last night. Such downright brazenness was the talk of the town. To think he had the brass to presume a squaw was worth five dollars.
- Lord Herrington surprised his stomach last Tuesday by drinking water.
- "Will There be Whiskey in Hell?" will be the text of the Reverend Theobold Jasper next Sunday. Many of our leading citizens are deeply interested in this question and a good attendance is expected.

## Prospecting on the Papago Reservation

Angie confessed to never being able to completely shake her love of all things having to do with mining, a carry-over from childhood and Wickenburg days. Always, she remained attuned to mining developments in the districts south of Casa Grande—the Silver Bell, as well as the Jackrabbit, the Copperosity, and the Orizaba, all on the Papago Reservation, where non-Indians could stake claims until 1955. Prospectors frequently went directly to the *Dispatch* to show off their ore samples, knowing that a receptive audience awaited them there. These prospectors told Angie about other sites on the reservation that contained a soft, red, decomposed rock that carried coarse gold.

This news traveled fast, so Angie and her associates, calling themselves the Indian Head Miners, hurriedly put together a prospecting trip to the reservation. Angie, Marvin, Clara Myers, her son and his wife, Ray and Alice Myers, Herman Veith, Josephine Jacobson, Stella and Ira Wagnon, and Howard

Snyder joined this prospecting venture. After establishing a camp on the reservation, all the women, except Josephine, returned to town.

The Indian Head Miners combed the hills nearby and stumbled across several reddish outcrops that looked as if rock had melted and run down a hillside. Excitement invariably gave way to disappointment when exploration of the underlying vein showed it to narrow and disappear completely down-dip.

Meanwhile, the camp's lone female soon tired of sleeping in the open and hiding behind mesquite bushes to dress. With the help of Herman Veith, Josephine cut long ocotillo branches and wired them together to form an enclosure. They then covered this thorny five-by-seven-foot bedroom with a wagon sheet for a roof and a blanket sheet for the door. Josephine blissfully bedded down for the night.

Marvin and Ira Wagnon hatched a plot to disrupt Josephine's slumber. Early the next morning, Marvin reached inside her cubicle and planted a tin can on the corner of Josephine's cot. Outside, Ira loudly proclaimed his prowess with a rifle. "Why I can even shoot that can off'n Jo's cot there!" He shot into the air. At that exact moment, Marvin reached inside the cubicle and knocked the can to the ground, hoping it would sound like a rifle shot.

Instead of reacting the way Marvin and Ira thought she would, Josephine sat up, looked around, and calmly reached under her pillow. She pointed a pistol first at Ira and then at Marvin. "I think your hats will make fine targets."

As she fired off a few warning shots, the men scrambled to get out of range. Josephine's camp status climbed a few notches that morning.

One evening Josephine and Herman Veith returned to camp after making a quick trip to Tucson. As proof that something besides cactus had been blooming on the desert, they produced a marriage license. From that moment on, fellow argonauts vowed no peace or privacy for the newlyweds in their ocotillo cubicle. Marvin tied a cowbell under Josephine's cot.

Marvin discovered a bee cave in Steamboat Mountain and rushed back with the news. "The honeycombs are so big they look like rock formations, just hanging there in plain sight. Can't you just taste that honey on our biscuits in the morning?"

Josephine produced a veil or two, and the beehive raiders tied strings to secure their clothing at ankles and wrists. When they got to the cave, they found the combs sandwiched between rock crevices — not quite as accessible as Marvin had made them out to be. After the carefully garbed raiders took a few jabs at the combs with shovels, huge armies of angry bees filled the mouth of the cave, and the honey thieves retreated to plan a new strategy.

Someone suggested a stick of dynamite to make the bees leave their honeycombs. As it turned out, the bees did leave. After the blast, the bees chased the hapless robbers all the way back to camp.

Tweezers and baking soda replaced picks and drills, while Marvin's popularity rating took a nosedive.

At some point Angie fell under the spell of Frank Picone, a capable mine engineer, and invested in Picone's primary prospect, the Aeolian Mine at the north end of the Santa Rosa Mountains. She became the company secretary and put considerable time into advertising for stockholders. Picone's daughter, Katherine, came to Casa Grande to live with Angie while she attended high school.

Picone brought in mining men to look over the Aeolian Mining Company's claims, including such experts as Hoval Smith, Parker Woodman, and General John C. Greenway. These engineers also looked at the area where the Indian Head group had been prospecting and agreed that the underlying rock formations might hold copper deposits. With the news that the district might host a big copper property, the Indian Head miners dug location holes with renewed spirit and energy, theorizing that if a big company came in to develop the property, they would want plenty of ground. Soon there were more than a hundred claims.

That theory paid off. General John Greenway, the much-celebrated mining engineer who had developed a means of extracting and processing ore at the New Cornelia Mine in Ajo, sent word to Picone that he would open up the Indian Head district. Greenway had already instructed Jim Megson to begin hauling in equipment from the New Cornelia Mine and said that development would begin when he returned from a business trip to the East. The mountaintops rang with the elated shouts of the Indian Head crew as they broke camp to return to town.

But Aeolus, the Greek ruler of the winds, chose to blow ill fortune on both the Indian Head prospect and the mining company that bore his name. Copper prices tumbled to nine cents in 1922, forcing Mr. Picone to suspend operations and begin selling off equipment and buildings at the Aeolian Mine. In

Angie's house in Casa Grande, built from Aeolian Mine lumber. Note the water tank and the rock pillars for the porch under construction. Tin Can Mansion lies behind the house.

order for Angie to recover some of her investment, Picone suggested that she salvage the lumber in the cook shack for a more comfortable home in Casa Grande.

Bill and Marvin spent a week at the mine dismantling the cook shack and cleaning up its lumber. Louie borrowed a FWD-Quad chain-drive truck from the Montizona Mine to haul the material into town. Just as he reached the road fronting the Tin Can Mansion with this unwieldy load, a wooden stringer that supported the truck bed snapped. All the building materials for Angie's new house slid into the street and had to be carried piece by piece onto the construction site.

In due time, this salvaged lumber grew into quite a respectable three-room house, complete with a rock fireplace and a front porch with stone pillars. Just up the street, a state-of-the-art high school was under construction.

When General Greenway died in New York, the dreams of the Indian Head miners died with him. All that remained were these memories of camp life on the Papago Reservation and a house for Angie.

Angie and her three sons. Left to right, they are Marvin, Bill, and Louie.

## Farewell to the *Dispatch*

Angie began questioning her sanity toward the end of 1924. None of her sons was interested in printing or newspaper publishing. Marvin took a job as a mechanic in a Phoenix creamery, and Bill worked with his uncle Charles Tweed as a plumber in Los Angeles. Louie and Bud's automotive repair business continued to flourish. Angie asked herself why she continued with the *Dispatch* when her sons had no interest in it.

The *Dispatch*'s current editor, Harold Wrenn, had served an apprenticeship with Angie. Unlike her sons, the young man seemed to like newspaper work, and he happened to be the son of A. C. Wrenn, publisher of the *Blade-Tribune* in Florence. It didn't take long for Angie to convince this father-son combo to buy the *Dispatch*. After twenty-one years, her newspaper career seemed to be coming to an end.

Her farewell message read, in part:

> **As for myself, I have enjoyed the work even though it took me through troubled times and to the threshold of disaster. My faith in the valley has been unfailing and my goal has been the winning of the San Carlos Dam and other developments in the valley.**
>
> **Now I'm ready to bend my efforts along other lines of endeavor, which have been beckoning for a long time.**

# NINE

## ～ To the Source It Returns

THE FIRST OF Angie's new endeavors began when she greeted Katharine MacRae with a hug, glad to see this very talented woman, now the wife of the mysterious man who had written "The Secret Plan" for the *Dispatch* so long ago. Katharine told Angie all about her appointment as manager of the Arizona Pageantry Association and her plans to stage one of these big, outdoor musical extravaganzas at the Casa Grande Ruins in November of 1926.

Angie smiled knowingly. "I'm not surprised to hear this. When the Casa Grande and Florence Women's Clubs met at the ruins with Frank Pinkley back in 1922, we talked about the idea of a pageant as a way to help publicize the monument and raise money for its protection. Do you know who's writing the script?"

Katharine curtsied. "I'm proud to announce that the script is in the hands of Byron Cummings, an archaeologist and the director of the Arizona State Museum. It will be a fanciful extravaganza with lots of dancing and warfare over lovely Indian maidens. The Casa Grande Women's Club has promised to make all the costumes. Now I just need you, Angie, to lend a hand with publicity."

Angie ended up working on the pageant for almost a whole year. She capitalized on the nation's curiosity about Arizona and the wild west. In the last-minute flurry of press releases, a letter arrived from Alvin Mills of the *Arizona Messenger* in Phoenix.

Wanting to retire, Mr. Mills asked if Angie would like to buy his weekly newspaper. The *Messenger* enjoyed a rich history of Democratic Party activism, first published as *El Mensajero* in 1900 for the Hispanic community. If Angie and her sons were interested, he would offer easy terms.

Oh, the possibilities! The letter revived Angie's most cherished dream—that of turning a newspaper dynasty over to her sons. As she wrote Bill and Marvin to tell them of the offer, she tried not to sound too hopeful.

Neither son answered in the affirmative but said they would be home soon to attend the pageant and spend Thanksgiving in Casa Grande.

### The Casa Grande Pageant

The extravaganza at the Casa Grande Ruins attracted thirteen thousand people from all parts of the country. They came by car and by special Southern Pacific trains. Automobiles parked anywhere and everywhere while thousands of people climbed all over the fragile ruins. With no seating provided, the audience sat upon the ground to watch the dramas staged on and around a wooden, multiple-story building, painted to resemble Compound B of the ruins.

The performance began with a corn dance in honor of the Sun God and a fair maiden dedicated to be the deity's sacred bride. People at the Casa Grande Pueblo succumbed to the charms of a handsome and clever stranger who taught them to gamble and play, instead of tending to their crops. The stranger then ran off with the Bride of the Sun. This caused such a curse of famine and disease to fall upon the village that not even later invaders could live there.

Generations later, Chief Morning Glow of Sacaton told his people:

> The land is all ours. It is a fair land and productive; but drought, and famine, and disease have evidently destroyed most of the people. The river has cut its channel so deep and changed its course so much that the intakes of the canals now lie far above and away from the water. We have found a place by a rocky ridge up the stream where we can build a dam and raise the water high enough to run it out into canals by which we can bring the water onto the lands along both sides of the Gila. Probably in time we shall find several such places.

The Indians then struggled against the Apaches, who killed their chief and carried away their women and corn. Other tribes came to the aid of the Indians and rescued their women. The pageant ended with a happy marriage ceremony.

Although the performances shed little light on the real history of the ancient people who had built the Casa Grande Pueblo, they did succeed in bringing the public's attention to the present plight of the Pimas and Papagos. The pageant at the ruins became an annual event until the depression years forced it into retirement.

## Dams and Canals but Still No Water

By the time Chief Morning Glow had uttered his words on stage in 1926, two diversion dams, the Sacaton and the Ashurst-Hayden, had been constructed on the Gila River to raise its water high enough to run into canals. But these dams and canals only allowed some big speculators to cash out and a few settlers to farm. Off to the southwest of the Gila, Casa Grande's irrigation district remained dry. The long-sought Ashurst-Hayden Diversion Dam allowed even less water to reach the tiny ten-acre fields allotted to each Indian by the government. However, Dr. Chandler's influence in Congress enabled him to get a road built across the top of the Sacaton Dam to give his guests at the San Marcos Hotel easy access to the Casa Grande Ruins.

## Young Stock Coming On

During the holidays, Bill received a Christmas card from his friend Frank Davis and was puzzled to read congratulations on his family's new venture into the publishing and printing business. Since Aunt Addie worked as the *Messenger*'s business manager, she doubtless had passed on her hope that Angie would buy the *Messenger*. But the Christmas card did motivate Bill into giving the matter more serious thought. Did he want to be a plumber or a printer? Marvin, too, admitted that he missed working on presses. Lengthy discussions ensued.

Angie told them, "If you're really interested, you must agree to come in as equal partners, for better or for worse." In weighing this decision, the threesome visited the *Messenger* plant at 37 West Jefferson in Phoenix.

Marvin's knees buckled at first sight of the Cranston Press, almost as large as a locomotive. He'd not had experience with anything larger than the *Dispatch*'s Diamond press, which would fit on the bed of a pickup truck.

While showing the Hammers around his plant, Mr. Mills took Angie aside. "I should warn you that some of the state's Democrats are not well pleased with the paper coming into the hands of a woman — and not a young woman to boot."

A. S. Mills watches Frank Lovett feed sheets of newsprint into a cylinder press at the First Avenue and Jefferson plant in Phoenix in 1926.

Angie bristled. "For the last twenty years, I've been hearing that women are not fit to run newspapers. What did you tell them?"

"I told them to have no apprehension because the young stock is coming on to take over when you're out of the picture."

That did it for Angie. She could never resist a challenge. "Thanks for your vote of confidence," she replied facetiously.

Angie and her two sons took over the *Messenger* in December of 1926, and Addie remained on as business manager. Other than Tillman Roberts, a young printer who had worked for John Driggs across the street, it was a family-run business in every sense of the word.

Each day Tillman approached the plant's old Linotype with a scowl on his face, while Marvin tinkered and coaxed the worn-out machine into submission. Angie crossed her fingers but soon realized that, in addition to the ten-thousand-dollar debt on the paper, she had to scare up even more money for equipment. She wrote,

> It was patent that I had to give the boys a firm foundation on which to work, so I borrowed money on the note I received in payment for the homestead. That gave us the wherewithal to get a brand new Model E Merganthaler Linotype.

The plant also needed a job press for contract printing, so to compensate for the other expenditure, she bought an old junk heap of a job press that Marvin managed to weld and retool. This job press came in handy for cartoon printing and a large run of envelopes for Governor Hunt.

No sooner had the Merganthaler been installed with great effort than the Hammers were told that the whole plant had to be moved to make way for the new Luhrs' Tower. Angie noted,

> George Luhrs let us have a room with an alley entrance to his existing building until more spacious quarters became available. Lawyers who came to us with legals to be published would have to pick their way through the alley, stepping over lumber and debris.

Eventually the plant moved out of these cramped conditions into more respectable quarters, and the *Messenger*'s volume of printing business increased. This necessitated the purchase of a three-thousand-dollar Miller high-speed press, but there was no place to put it. Angie announced another move in a 1931 edition of the *Messenger*:

**Saturday, April 18, marks another milestone in the progressive history of the
*Messenger*.**

**Today we are moving our entire printing plant and business office to the
building known as the Arizona Fire Building, Second Avenue and Adams. We
have leased the entire basement, which will more than double our present ca-
pacity and provide additional floor space for our further development of an
afternoon daily Democrat paper.**

**By working all day Sunday with a force of men, we anticipate being ready for
business Monday morning in our new location. Opposite the Orpheum theater, the plant will be more centralized and of greater convenience to the public.
This expansion was only finally determined after weeks of consideration and
a firm belief in the future of Phoenix.**

With Angie at the helm, the *Phoenix Messenger* became the *Arizona Messenger*. Her twenty-eight years of newspaper experience, combined with firsthand knowledge of communities, mining, agriculture, and politics, resulted
in a mature, well-balanced paper covering news throughout the entire state.
Angie was at her prime. Although still a weekly, the *Messenger* became such
a driving force that its owners began toying with the idea of turning it into
a daily.

## The Colorado River Controversy

Angie worked hard to stay abreast of water developments throughout the state,
examining every copy of the *Congressional Record* and filing it for future refer-
ence. She knew all the principal players in the Gila River Irrigation Project and
the state's fight for the waters of the Colorado River. Hardly a single edition
of the *Messenger* went to press without water news of some kind. She considered it her sacred duty to inform the public on these matters as she gained
increasingly more information and perspective.

One of her favorite informants since *Dispatch* days was Senator Fred Colter
from Apache County, a man she held in high esteem for his knowledge of
water law. Colter couldn't let go of the vision he had inherited from his mentor,
George Maxwell, the founder of the National Reclamation Association. This
vision encompassed bringing water from the Colorado River across 470 miles
of rugged terrain to irrigate desert lands in the central region of Arizona. They

called this plan the High Line Canal, and though few people took it seriously, Colter filed for power and dam sites along the river. Angie loved a visionary. She wrote,

> **When we took over the *Messenger*, I spent hours on end trying to figure out what Colter meant to say in the information he gave me. Henry L. Mencken [a prominent political commentator and journalist at the time] once wrote an article about Colter, referring to his mode of speaking as "Navajo English." It was remarkable how well Colter could visualize what he wanted to say, but had difficulty putting it into words. When he married Dorothy, she took over the editing of his articles and did a fine piece of work with them.**

The controversy over California's efforts to construct Boulder Dam across the Colorado River was under way, as was the issue of whether the Colorado River Compact should be ratified. This compact, an agreement between the seven states that shared drainage into the river, seemed reasonable when drawn up in 1922. It divided the Colorado water equally between the Upper Basin states of Wyoming, Colorado, Utah, and New Mexico, and the Lower Basin states of California, Nevada, and Arizona.

However, the compact didn't specify the amount of water that was to be shared, and now it seemed the Reclamation Service sided with California's efforts to secure support for Boulder, a storage and hydroelectric dam across the river. A total of 580 miles of the Colorado flows within or along Arizona's boundary, while California contributed the least in drainage and stood to benefit the most from construction of such a dam. Enactment of the Boulder Canyon legislation would mean approval of the Colorado River Contract and authorization of an All-American Canal that would carry the Colorado's water into southern California farmlands. Angie remembered,

> **In one of the issues of the *Congressional Record*, there appeared a map of Indian lands near Yuma. Two hundred and seventy-five thousand acres of this land was all that was to be allotted to the state after the building of Boulder Dam in the Swing-Johnson Bill. I was so incensed at this bold thievery of Arizona's greatest asset that I immediately began a series of editorials and articles about the injustice of the proposition.**
>
> **If Fred Colter's filings had been upheld by the state as they should have been, our position would have been invincible, despite the federal withdrawal**

**of lands along the Colorado River in 1904. I have copies of a Supreme Court decision that Arizona could build dams and irrigation works above Boulder Dam and the government was required to grant rights-of-way. Not even our lawmakers would turn a hand to help Colter hold the filing he had made for the state. Instead, they reviled him for his efforts.**

Angie stood squarely behind Governor Hunt's position on the issue and found herself roundly criticized by some Democrats for giving Fred Colter, a Republican, so much airtime in the *Messenger*.

In 1928, during the most intense phase of this controversy, a tall, handsome man came to the *Messenger* looking for work and introduced himself as a former publisher of the *Owens Valley Herald* in Inyo County, California. He handed Angie a set of photos from his briefcase that showed prosperous-looking homes nestled amid lush farm fields. "This is how our valley looked before the Los Angeles Metropolitan Water District went to work on it." He then produced another set of pictures showing skeletal trees and deteriorating homes surrounded by barren fields of stubble. "This is how it looks now."

Angie looked up from the pictures to study the man's face. "Now I know who you are. You're Harry Glasscock, the man who led the water fight between the people of Owens Valley and the City of Los Angeles. Are you serious about working here at the *Messenger*?"

"Absolutely. That fight has left me homeless, divorced, and destitute. I want to let the people of Arizona know what's in store for them if the avariciousness of Los Angeles isn't stopped right now."

Harry Glasscock's voice crackled with anger as he recounted the tale of how L.A.'s two-hundred-mile aqueduct transported water out of the Owens River and dried up their valley. "Insiders who knew where the aqueduct would be built bought huge tracts of barren land in the San Fernando Valley for practically nothing. When the aqueduct brought water, they turned around and sold this land for thousands of dollars an acre." As if trying to shut out the memory, he tossed the pictures into his briefcase and snapped it shut with finality.

Of course, Angie gave this veteran water warrior a desk and advanced him money, and Glasscock began cranking out a series of articles for the *Messenger*. The first, entitled "The Fight at the Water Hole," outlined the history of water in the West and asked a rhetorical question: Should the resources of any given section of the country be subservient to the political and commercial desires of a stronger section?

In another article, "Dynamite Fans Flames in Water Struggle against Powerful City," Glasscock described how a group of Owens County settlers placed a charge of dynamite under the aqueduct one night in 1924. When the Los Angeles City Council offered a reward of ten thousand dollars for the arrest and conviction of the guilty parties, 187 men from Owens Valley confessed to the crime. L.A. detectives had to return home empty-handed. Glasscock went on to write:

> My interest in this matter is merely that which any normal human might feel for another. We of Owens Valley have gone through this fire. We know what it is, and if we can keep another country from suffering a like fate, we have done something worthwhile. Suicides and broken homes have been but highlights in this destruction of Owens Valley by Los Angeles. The friends of years have been separated and made to go among strangers to begin life over again.

Angie watched Harry spiral into hopeless depression. Even putting his name below hers as associate editor of the *Messenger* didn't help. He carried a gold pocket watch, a going-away present inscribed with the names of his "monkey wrench" confederates. Each morning he came to work with alcohol on his breath, opened his watch, and after placing it beside his typewriter, let it tick away the hours of his life.

Against Arizona's objections, the Boulder Canyon Project Act passed Congress in 1928, and work began on that massive structure across the Colorado that would be renamed Hoover Dam. The Reclamation Service planned another huge undertaking when, and if, Arizona ratified the Colorado River Compact. That undertaking, called the Central Arizona Project, was to be modeled after Colter and Maxwell's dream of a High Line Canal with an aqueduct to carry water from the Colorado River to central Arizona. But before Congress would approve this Central Arizona Project, Arizona and California had to resolve their differences over the division of water, a tug of war over which state would have the biggest farms or the biggest cities. Arizona didn't ratify the Colorado River Compact until 1944.

In 1929, Glasscock left suddenly for Los Angeles. While there, he ended his life. Angie mourned the passing of this fellow publisher, whom she had so admired.

The *Bee-Messenger* and the Advertising Monopoly

In 1930 the *Arizona Republican* declared itself independent and, as Angie put it, "lopped the tail off its name to make it seem less partisan." Its owners bought out the Democratic *Evening Gazette*, and together these two entrenched Phoenix dailies advanced a partisan Republican agenda under control of the Arizona Publishing Company. Democratic Party loyalists watched the unfolding of these events with alarm, while the *Messenger* made plans to balance the playing field with a daily that was first called the *Arizona Evening Democrat*.

On January 24, 1931, the *Messenger* announced, "Tri-State Publishers Corporation Completes New Organization to Publish Snappy Daily Newspaper."

> Here is the big news of the day for Phoenix and the whole state of Arizona. After months of careful analysis and serious consideration, the *Messenger* owners decided that expansion was a necessity. Always strictly a Democratic paper and working for those principles, the owners, at the instigation of many prominent citizens decided to incorporate its rapidly growing printing and publishing business. This has just been completed with the Tri-State Publishers, Inc., with a capital stock of $300,000, a small amount of which will be open to public subscription as soon as the Corporation Commission issues the necessary permit.
>
> Hundreds of people have gone on record that Phoenix and Arizona must have an afternoon daily, independent, fearless, and standing for fair play as well as the upbuilding of our state. Along these lines, the new organization is conducting its expansion policy and nothing short of a cataclysm will stop the forward movement in the interest of all citizens and honest government.

A talented staff did, indeed, come together for the upcoming daily, and somewhere along the line, its name changed to the *Bee-Messenger*. With John Henry Whyte as Angie's co-editor and Bryan Akers as business manager, everyone waited for the depression clouds to lift. John Henry Whyte had been a former secretary to Governor Hunt, and Bryan was the son of Charles Akers, who had owned the *Phoenix Gazette* before it was sold. Bryan contracted for a high-speed duplex press as his contribution to the concern, and Dick Smith functioned as circulation manager. With a power press and the International News Service at their disposal, this gifted staff waited to launch their tabloid.

In April of 1932, President Hoover announced that a turning point in the depression had been reached, and the nation was on the road to economic recovery. The *Bee-Messenger*'s staff rolled out its first edition, which hit the streets for three cents a copy right before the depression's really black days. Angie later remembered,

> **Jack Stewart, our reporter and now a hotel tycoon, had an uncanny knack for uncovering both good and bad news. We printed both kinds of news, sometimes to our regret, but we checked every item for accuracy before we printed it.**
>
> **I was so accustomed to thinking in terms of weekly newspapers that I let a scoop on the kidnapping of the Lindbergh baby pass by. We had time to break the story first but were so shocked by the crime that we waited for more news to come in.**

When a prominent physician was arrested for selling drugs, the *Bee-Messenger* ran the story after checking with law enforcement, while other Phoenix papers kept silent about the case. Angie, John Henry Whyte, and Jack Stewart debated whether newspapers should be charged as accessories to a crime if they covered up criminal actions.

Unfortunately, the *Bee-Messenger* didn't get the unanimous support from Democratic Party members that Angie and her staff believed they would have. Some of those Democrats had ambitions of starting their own paper and even tried to discourage Governor Hunt from supporting the *Bee-Messenger*.

Angie and her staff couldn't have chosen a worse time to launch their daily. The depression hit Arizona later than in the eastern part of the nation, so for a while, the baby tabloid floated on fumes as Bryan Akers canvassed the business community to pick up a few nickels in advertising. That's when he discovered that most of the merchants had signed contracts with the *Republic and Gazette* syndicate. "It's a nasty business," one merchant told Bryan. "If we use any other paper for advertising, we'll have to pay higher costs per inch for future ads in the *Republic*. Even though we want to give you our business, we can't afford to."

The *Bee-Messenger* died in its infancy at the age of six months, and the Hammers returned to printing and publishing the weekly *Arizona Messenger*.

Still smarting from the *Republic*'s stranglehold on Phoenix merchants, Angie became her firm's designated representative to the Phoenix Chamber of Commerce. There, she joined a committee who called themselves the Arizona Advertisers' Club. This committee began an investigation of fraudulent advertising schemes in the city.

Meanwhile, Anna Boettiger, Eleanor and Franklin Roosevelt's daughter, tried to establish another Democratic newspaper in Phoenix. Earl Zarbin, the author of *All the Time a Newspaper: The First Hundred Years of the Arizona Republic*, tells about Anna Boettiger's short newspaper career and how she tried to help the Advertisers' Club:

> It was in the midst of these harder business times that a new daily newspaper began in Phoenix. It was the *Arizona State Democrat*, and, in its short life, October 18 — November 20, may have been most notable for a two-line banner October 23: Merchants War on Ad Monopoly. According to the story below the headline, the advertising monopoly was the combined *Republic and Gazette*. The story said that seventy-six leading merchants of Phoenix last night formed the Arizona Advertiser's Club. War was declared upon the monopoly of this city by one newspaper organization [the Arizona *Messenger*]. The article showed that ad rates had risen in the eleven months since the papers joined.

However, Anna Boettiger's paper didn't fail because of the depression or lack of party support. It failed because her business manager disappeared along with her paper's bank account.

Smarting from the failure of both daily papers, Angie threw all her resources into the Advertisers' Club and its effort to break the advertising monopoly of the large Phoenix papers. She wrote to Mr. M. R. Pratt of the *Los Angeles Evening Herald Express* about the problem, hoping that a little out-of-state adverse publicity might stir things up a bit. Among other things, she told Mr. Pratt that the *Republic*'s policy was a violation of the Sherman Anti-trust Law and that she had talked to Sidney P. Osborn about sponsoring a bill to make Arizona advertising laws conform to federal advertising laws. Mr. Pratt duly published an article on the subject in his Los Angeles paper. Soon after, the *Republic* syndicate changed its policy, and most fraudulent advertising schemes disappeared from the valley.

### The Committee of Six

Flushed with this success, certain members of the Advertisers' Club decided they would remain together and change their name to the "Committee of Six," with the lofty goal of finding a solution to the nation's economic woes. Angie wrote, "We all wondered why we had to have such critical times when our country was so rich. There needed to be some way of driving poverty from our land."

This committee began screening various monetary plans being promoted by different people and groups around the country. Most of these plans called for the use of scrip, or government-issued paper money, as a medium of exchange for labor and products. The committee then reported the most promising plans they reviewed to the chamber of commerce board of directors. Angie wrote,

> **One of those plans developed by a Utah bartering group met with approval from the board. The only person in the group to speak against this plan was a minister who thought it would hurt business. Most of us were under the impression that there was no business to hurt at the time.**
>
> **It was then that Technocracy blazed across the country and looked as though it might be the solution of our national problems.**

Angie embraced the movement with characteristic fervor. The Technocrats sought to replace the gold standard with government-issued scrip for every man, woman, and child in the country, thus leveling the economic playing field and erasing poverty. So eager was Angie to share this revelation with the public that she splashed Technocracy all over the front page of the *Messenger*, even suggesting that the Democratic Party embrace the concept in its platform. She recollected,

> **Afterwards, I learned that political parties were absolutely taboo in the Technocracy set-up. I found, too, that any suggestion of such a change in our monetary system automatically put the person suggesting it in the category of subversive or Communist, though it would be hard to find a more loyal and patriotic group than the Technocrats. They just didn't have the right leadership to satisfy rank and file members who wanted a constitution to conform with our national constitution.**

Contract printing allowed the Hammers to remain halfway solvent during the depression years. They took over the contract for Bryan Akers' Duplex press, which made it possible to print eight-column, four-page circulars for business firms, small-town newspapers, and magazines. For a while, they published a little *Phoenix Shopping News* tabloid on a twice-weekly basis, but without the capital to hang on, this venture, too, collapsed. However, the commercial printing arm of the concern flourished in such a way that Angie could turn her attention to relatives living in Wickenburg.

## A Heart Divided

The Hassayampa had lured back all of the former Hutchinson sisters except Monica and Angie by the late 1920s. Addie had quit working for the *Messenger* and built a house on a hilltop close to town where she cared for her ailing ex-husband, Charles Tweed. Gen and Veva moved into Sarah's old house, adjacent to the Bar FX Ranch, and Pattie played hostess to dudes after F.X. died in 1926.

Pattie never knew how many people would be seated around her big dining room table. Large hunks of beef hung in her kitchen cold box while a fresh pot of pinto beans bubbled away on the cookstove. The big, primitive rock fireplace in the living room, surrounded by Indian baskets, war bonnets, tomahawks, and collections of arrowheads, looked as if it had seen centuries of cave dwellers. Here in this relaxed atmosphere, guests had no doubt they were experiencing a slice of the Old West.

Angie, Bill, and Marvin spent Christmas Day at the ranch with family and guests in 1931, where they reminisced about F. X. O'Brien. His last charitable act had been to donate a five-acre tract of land to the Wickenburg School District for a high school. Angie voiced her dismay that not even a street in the whole town had been named after her generous brother-in-law.

Pattie shared her last memory of F.X. "He threw the covers off his bed, swung his legs over the edge, and stood up, saying that he just wanted to throw his feet over the dashboard one more time. After that, he collapsed to the floor and died."

As often happens at such gatherings, talk turned to stories of the old days. When the Hammers returned to Phoenix, Angie wrote an article about one of these stories for the New Year's edition of the *Arizona Messenger*:

**REMINISCENCES**
**The Messenger family spent Christmas day in Wickenburg with friends and relatives and took occasion to let them all see copies of the paper. The "Remi-**

A surrey shuttles guests to the Bar FX Guest Ranch in Wickenburg. Tony O'Brien is on the horse at right.

niscences" had the effect of bringing out more and more of the stories of long ago, especially in Phoenix. W.A. Farish, now engineer for the Whitman interests who are building the Walnut Grove project, was there. Mr. Farish told of the first Phoenix jail and lamented the fact that proper steps had not been taken to preserve the most unique relic imaginable.

The first jail was an immense log of wood to which prisoners were chained. The log was discarded when two prisoners just recovering from a protracted spree found themselves driven to distraction for a drink. Not being able to disengage themselves from the log, they took the "jail" with them to the Fender Saloon, located where the Phoenix National Bank now stands. Fender had just installed a new bar and was quite proud of his new furnishings. Knowing this, the prisoners asked for drinks. Upon his refusal, they threatened to scratch the new bar with the "jail" if he failed. On condition that they would leave with the jail and not come back, they obtained the drink.

This kind of a portable jail proved very unsatisfactory, so the officers obtained an immense river boulder weighing about half a ton to which was attached a strong iron ring to which prisoners were chained. This served as a jail for many years. Many old-timers will remember the boulder. It lay around Phoenix for years, and the last time it was seen by Mr. Farish was about twenty years ago, near Five Points in the old canal. It has probably buried itself in the mud where it may never be found. This would have been a valuable addition to the museum.

### The Pioneer Play at Wickenburg

At some time in the early 1930s, Pattie lamented to Angie, "There is so much infighting among our many guest ranches jockeying for position in the dude trade that it has brought strife to the whole social and business structure of Wickenburg."

Calling to mind the reason she left Wickenburg in the first place, this was the last thing that Angie wanted to hear. But basking in the success of the pageant at the Casa Grande Ruins, she offered Pattie a different solution than the one she had chosen when she decided to leave Wickenburg in 1912. "I can see no reason for people in this charming town to be at sword's point all the time. If they could come together on a big project and become better acquainted, they would surely see each other as fine people."

Angie, Pattie, Gen, and Addie huddled together to mull over the possibility of a town pageant, and all agreed that Wickenburg contained enough raw talent to pull it off. Soon the idea steamrolled through town, and volunteers began signing up to become actors and actresses or to make costumes for the play. Angie began outlining the script.

The usual naysayers came forward to voice doubts. How could novices such as themselves hope to stage such an event without the services of a costly, high-powered director? Angie's answer was to go directly to Ray Myers, Clara Myers' son, in Casa Grande. Ray had been a pioneer in the early days of Hollywood's moving-picture industry, a top director for D. W. Griffith, the producer of "Birth of the Nation." Ray agreed to direct the pageant for a nominal fee and took Angie's outline and research notes for study. She wrote,

**Mrs. Mike Echeverria made skilled and beautiful Spanish dancers out of young people who had never taken dancing lessons. William O. Bass took the part of Tah-Ask, the Sun God and supervised the Indian dance ceremonies.**

After untold hours and many months of preparation, the actual work of plowing seats into a hillside overlooking a small valley on the Bar FX Ranch began in 1934. Stage settings that replicated old stores, dance halls, and saloons took shape at various locations up and down the valley. The performance was to be staged at night under large spotlights playing from one set to another. A. F. Moriarty of the Central Arizona Light and Power Company hooked up floodlights and masterminded the lighting. Harvey Mott of the *Arizona Republic* promoted the event in Phoenix newspapers.

Pattie's youngest son, Tony, took the part of a frontiersman in a wagon train. On the second night of the performance, a misplaced stage light blinded Tony's horse as he rode across the stage with a fake arrow in his back. The horse bolted, bucked Tony off, then broke through a protective barrier and straddled the lap of a woman in the audience. Amid the ensuing pandemonium, Ray rushed over to the lady and Angie hurried to her nephew, fearing the worst until she saw Tony's laughing face appear over the side of the horse. Neither horse nor spectator was injured in the mishap, and the latter refused to go to a doctor because she wanted to see the rest of the play.

Angie felt satisfied that the pageant had accomplished its goal of bringing people together to celebrate their town's history. She wrote,

**While the play was a loss financially, it more than justified its presentation by the great improvement in the town's social structure through the associations during the training period.**

Years later, Sophie Burden, long-time proprietor of the Remuda Ranch in Wickenburg, became a columnist for the *Wickenburg Sun*. In one of her columns, she reflected on her memories of the first pioneer play:

> The play, written by A. H. Hammer, had four acts. The first was "Indians and Immigrants" and was the most impressive. Bill Bass was the Indian medicine man, the voice of Tah Ask. The second act was "Wickenburg: the Discovery of the Vulture Mine" or "A Jackass May be Man's Best Friend." Act three was "Pinole Treaty: Who Said Treachery?" Act four was "Fiesta: Arrival of the First Santa Fe Train."
>
> The pageant was cleverly and beautifully done. Unfortunately, I don't believe it paid for itself, which was too bad. That was possibly because practically everyone in town was involved in it one way or another, leaving no one for the audience. Too, it was right after the Depression, and people were not driving much.

## The Pieces of Her Life

Although the *Arizona Messenger* had limped through the depression, the newspaper itself returned little, if any, financial gain to its owners. With the *Messenger* in the hands of her capable sons, Bill and Marvin, Angie had more time to devote to community and state affairs. She served on the State Board of Social Security and Welfare until 1943 and played active roles in her two favorite organizations, the Phoenix Business and Professional Women and the Phoenix Pen Women's Association. The latter group encouraged her to begin writing her memoirs. With pieces of her past scattered among Wickenburg, Phoenix, and Casa Grande, Angie began rounding up memories and keeping a diary of her activities.

In Casa Grande, Louie had long since married Anna Margaret Peck, a former high school English teacher and daughter of the town mayor. With one young son and another baby on the way, Louie and Margaret added more rooms to the old house built with lumber from the Aeolian Mine.

As the automotive business expanded, Louie and his partner, Bud Bottriell, bought a block of property on the outskirts of town where the Airdrome had been located. There, they built a modern service station, automotive repair shop, and hardware store, complete with pots and pans and sporting goods. Far from the original commercial district along the railroad, they enticed other businessmen to join them by building to suit the needs of tenants. They constructed a new post office and leased it to the government for a dollar a year and even finagled Harry Nace, the builder of the Orpheum Theatre in Phoenix, to construct an almost equally elaborate movie theater across from their B & L Supply store. Main Street moved away from the railroad tracks and closer to "Bud and Louieville" on Florence Street.

Ted Healey waited until he was sure that Angie wouldn't return to Casa Grande before selling the *Bulletin* to the *Dispatch* in 1928. Today, the *Dispatch* retains its legacy of independent ownership in the hands of the Donovan Kramer family.

In 1938, Louie's wife, Margaret, died from complications brought about by misdiagnosed "summer complaint," which was in reality a torn appendix that slowly leaked poison into her bloodstream. Angie then found herself playing the role of surrogate mother to Louie's young children, Donald and Betty. That same year, she sold the *Arizona Messenger* to Mr. Charles Wilson so that she could devote more of her time to family.

Whether Ted Healey ever accepted that "good little women" had the ability to run a newspaper remains uncertain, but for a while, it did look as if he was winning the dispute with Angie over the best way to bring water and prosperity to the Casa Grande Valley.

Acreage devoted to the "white gold" of long-staple cotton tripled between the two world wars, just as Healey had hoped. Even the depression didn't have much of an effect on agriculture because the Valley National Bank loaned large sums of money to cotton farmers to keep them afloat. The farmers installed increasingly efficient pumping equipment in tube wells that reached deeper and deeper into the earth. Then construction began on the big dam that would supposedly bring to an end all the water woes of both Indians and non-Indians alike and double the size of the water users' Casa Grande–Florence Project.

In 1928, President Calvin Coolidge came to the dedication of this dam, whose name had been changed from the San Carlos to the Coolidge Dam as a political ploy to get him to endorse the project. Louie attended this dedication and described the "big wigs" seated at banquet tables across the top of the dam and his thrill at discovering Will Rogers quietly eating among the rest of the common folk. Called to join the president at the top of the dam, Will hung his head in an "aw, shucks" manner and scribed circles in the dirt with his shoe. After that, upon noting the green moss growing upon the lake backed up by the dam, he made the oft-repeated remark that if the lake was his, he'd mow it.

In her memoirs, Angie wrote poignantly of the struggle to bring the Coolidge Dam and its canals into existence:

> **Many new men and women came to the valley and joined in the fight, but the real oldsters who actually dug canals, plowed and irrigated land and made homes, laid the foundation. The tragedy of it all is that many fell by the wayside of poverty and heartbreak. They waited and waited for the dam but had to leave their homes and abandon all they had built before completion of the project. Those who held onto their land and came back later are now reaping the benefits of those pioneering efforts to bring water to the valley.**

As it turned out, neither Angie nor Ted Healey could feel completely vindicated by their divergent views on the development of the Casa Grande Valley. Angie had correctly upheld Dr. Smith's warning that the continual mining of underground aquifers would eventually deplete the valley's water supply and cause irrigated lands to return to desert. Pinal County's agricultural development slowed considerably when the cost of pumping the declining Pleistocene aquifers made farming less feasible. However, the great Coolidge Dam did not bring as much prosperity to farms watered by the San Carlos Irrigation Project as Angie had expected.

Current development of Pinal County comes from neither pumped groundwater nor a system of canals; it comes from beleaguered transplants driven from parts of the country with hostile winter environments. Today, row upon row of new housing developments stand in fields once devoted to "white gold."

Angie, Bill, and Marvin retained the Messenger Printing Company and moved it to a new location at 210 West Adams Street. With Bill as president and general manager, the company merged with Columbus Giragi's Arizona Printers and became the state's highest-volume and best-equipped printing

The *Messenger* plant at 210 West Adams in Phoenix.

firm. Marvin patented three different kinds of printing equipment as the industry evolved from hot lead to offset printing. Both sons married and gave Angie five more grandchildren.

Angie's sketchy notes about the fate of the *Wickenburg Miner* show that she had harbored hopes about returning to Wickenburg over the years.

> **The Halls published the *Miner* until some time in the summer of 1918 when Mrs. Hall had to give it up after Ernest volunteered for the Twenty-Seventh Engineers. [Apparently the paper had been leased to Dick Wick Hall's brother, Ernest, and his wife.] After the Halls came the Hawkins. I don't remember what kind of a deal I made with them. I was just glad to have someone to keep it alive until I could take over again. The last deal I remember was with Walter Martin, who moved the paper to Tempe, where it breathed its last breath when its files were lost in a fire.**

Angie continued living in Phoenix but shuttled back and forth between Wickenburg and Casa Grande on the Greyhound Bus. In Wickenburg, Angie and her sisters concentrated on writing. Angie continued working on her memoirs and swapping early memories with her sisters. Gen wrote short stories about Irish prospectors, then undertook a fictional epic novel about the migrations of the long-vanished Hohokam Indians. In early days, she had spent a lot of time at the Casa Grande Ruins with Frank Pinkley. Addie wrote a science fiction book for children, "The Adventures of Ollibolly the Moon Man." Olli had radio ears that allowed him to understand the languages of earth people, so he came to investigate the reasons for their bickering.

This period of creativity and watching over her flock of grandchildren spurred Angie into another campaign. As television became more accessible to households in the 1940s, there were no programs designed specifically for children, only reruns of old westerns and crime shows. Angie became concerned about the "type of mental food being fed our children by television," and she began writing letters to friends and associates like Anna Boettiger, hoping to interest them in setting up a corporation to produce programs for young viewers. As usual, she solicited the support of Ray Myers, who agreed to direct a series of Addie's Ollibolly adventures if Angie succeeded in establishing this corporation.

The more Angie spent time in Wickenburg, the more she wanted to live there permanently. When she discovered that the old Watson stock-raising

Angie's Wickenburg "igloo" in 1950.

homestead west of Wickenburg along Highway 60 was for sale, she bought it, intending to resell most of the acreage but retain a portion for a residence of her own. She observed,

> All that country was a series of rolling hills and the highway traversed a winding ridge that we used to call the "serpentine road." O.G. Jones was the first to do any extensive leveling of a large hill that filled adjacent hollows and made way for what is now the Double J Court. Mr. Jones thought I would be wise to level the land next to the Holmes service station. I had it leveled and sold it to Charles Winter.

Angie had a way of attracting visionaries into her life: this time an architect promoting the idea of dome homes. The architect drew up plans and began building, while relatives shook their heads in disbelief. Who but Angie would consider building an igloo with gothic arches? An alien-looking house took shape in a secluded arroyo.

Before Angie had time to complete her last three projects, the establishment of television programs for children, the completion of her dome home, and the compilation of her prodigious writing, she suffered a massive stroke.

Angie crossed over into the spirit realm in 1952. Among her papers, she left a poem by Ella Wheeler Wilcox that embodied Angie's philosophy of life and death:

*The Law*

You were, and you will be, know this while you are,
Your spirit has traveled both long and afar.
It came from the Source, to the Source it returns;
The spark that was lighted eternally burns.

It slept in the jewel. It leaped in the wave.
It roamed in the forest. It rose from the grave.
It took on strange garbs for long eons of years,
And now in the soul of your self it appears.

From body to body your spirit speeds on,
It seeks a new form when the old one is gone,
And the form that it finds is the fabric you wrought,
On the loom of the mind with the fiber of thought.

You are your own devil. You are your own God.
You fashion the paths that your footsteps have trod.
And no one can save you from error or sin,
Until you shall hark to the spirit within.

Once list to that voice and all tumult is done,
Your life is the life of the Infinite One.
In the hurrying race you are conscious of pause,
With Love for the purpose and Love for the cause.

## Conclusion

By the time of Angela's birth in 1870, women of the West had already begun venturing beyond the prescribed roles of housewife and mother. Angela's mother had homesteaded, taught school, administered frontier medicine, and displayed all the resiliency and self-sufficiency it took to survive and bear chil-

Angie at age seventy-six.

dren in remote mining camps. But Sarah couldn't break the bonds of conservative Victorian standards and Roman Catholic doctrine. It was up to Angela and the next generation of women to begin testing their talents and new ways of thinking. And so it continues as each preceding generation lays the groundwork.

In Angie's case, she went from riding sidesaddle (as "decent" women rode) to becoming a powerful force in the shaping of her communities and her state. But perhaps her most enduring trait was that, regardless of rascally men and greedy swindlers, she never lost faith in the innate goodness and fairness of ordinary people to put things right—"with Love for the purpose and Love for the cause."

# Appendix

### Setting the Record Straight

Angela included this account of Henry Wickenburg in her papers to "set the record straight."

Of all that I have heard and read about Henry's discovery of the Vulture, the only one that rings true is the version told by E.N. Rudd, a man who lived with Henry a good fifty years off and on. In the hope that history will eventually right itself, this is the interview with Mr. Rudd that appeared in the *Wickenburg Sun* in 1936.

"I have read several articles about Henry Wickenburg . . . how he discovered the Vulture, accounts of his fights with the Indians, and how he dug the tunnel through the hill for protection against them. At night, sitting before the fireplace, we talked about his early adventures and about the Indians. He told me he never had trouble with Indians in the early years, only later when other settlers came.

As to the discovery of the mine, it was when gold was discovered at Rich Hill. There were several men digging with Henry and with an absence of picks and shovels, they dug with butcher knives. For a period of eighteen days, the diggers averaged a hundred dollars each.

While the men camped there, a troop of cavalry under command of Major Van came across the country bound to Prescott from Yuma. The troop camped at the diggings overnight. They told Wickenburg of having run onto a campfire where several pack saddles had been burned. A lot of ore was scattered around like it had been dumped from sacks. The soldiers thought Indians had overtaken some prospector, burned his saddles and dumped the ore. The soldiers took some of this ore and it was, indeed, rich in gold. Before Wickenburg left, the soldiers pointed out the place where they had found the pack saddles as nearly as they could.

After the best of the gold was taken out of Rich Hill, Wickenburg and two other men came down to Wickenburg's spring. Camp was made there and the men rode out to try to find the burned pack saddles. They never located the fire nor any diggings.

After resting under an ironwood tree that stands near the present Vulture assay office, Wickenburg said he walked up the hill to about where the big cave was and picked up rock that looked good. He brought the rock back to the springs, panned it, and found it to be rich in gold.

Wickenburg and two of the men located three claims of a hundred feet. [This was before the enactment of the new law providing for 1,500-foot claims.] The two partners left, and Wickenburg stayed on to dig a cabin in the hill to the south of the tunnel. [This is the tunnel at the mine, not the one at Wickenburg.] Wickenburg dug out the ore and ground it with an arrastra. When the new law governing the size of claims was passed, Wickenburg relocated the claims, leaving out the names of the other partners.

Wickenburg told how a party came in and built a four-stamp mill near his house and constructed a road. He paid sixteen dollars a ton to have the ore hauled to the mill with ox teams. The ore was rich, and a lot of bullion was accumulated, but there was no money to pay the bills. The man in charge took the bullion out to exchange it for money but never returned. Wickenburg didn't know what became of him.

By this time, Wickenburg was in debt twenty-five thousand dollars, so he built several arrastras and with them milled about thirty thousand worth of gold. Then he bonded the claim for a hundred thousand and took fifteen thousand down with eighty-five thousand due at the maturity of the bond.

When Wickenburg went to claim his eighty-five thousand, he was told, 'You are paid in full.' He spent his remaining fifteen thousand on lawsuits to recover the balance, but to no avail. Mr. Wickenburg never did get any of the millions taken from the mine."

Angie wrote that Henry's mouth was twisted almost off the side of his face, as a result of having been shot in the face by an Apache. He grew a shaggy beard to cover this deformity and always dressed in the standard overalls and red flannel shirt of pioneers. "He was a friendly, garrulous man," she noted, "and old-timers often gathered to swap stories in his tiny hut. His pride and joy was his vegetable garden watered from a spring nearby."

Angie ended this treatise by saying that Henry killed several people he found stealing his vegetables. This, no doubt, would account for the seven lone graves on Boot Hill that she mentioned in connection with Wickenburg's funeral. There's no public record of these deaths.

## A Family Legend

Nora Hutchinson (Angela's grandmother) began life as Nora Coughlin of Westmeath County in Ireland around the turn of the nineteenth century. Little is known of her background, other than that she was said to have been beautiful and well educated. However, much is known of the man she married, Andrew Augustus O'Higgins, a first cousin to Bernardo O'Higgins, the liberator of Chile. Like Bernardo, Andrew Augustus seemed to possess a voracious appetite for adventure and exploration.

After graduating from Carrick McCross College as a civil engineer, Andrew took off for Australia with Nora. This was probably sometime between 1810 and 1815. The couple settled in Sydney, where Andrew built a fleet of three sailing ships and made a fortune in the import-export business. His success afforded an unusually luxurious lifestyle for Nora and their burgeoning Irish-Catholic family. The best scholars available in Australia tutored all six of their children.

Then, one after the other, Andrew's ships, the *Skern* and the *Trinkamalee*, fell prey to fierce storms at sea. When the only remaining ship, the *Sarah*, limped into port with its valuable cargo of linens intact, Andrew decided to join California's rush for gold to recoup his fortune. "You can sell enough of the *Sarah*'s cargo to keep going until I can send for you," Andrew told Nora.

After six months of waiting, Nora received a letter from Andrew. "Come on the first passenger ship bound for San Francisco. Let me know the name of your ship and I'll be waiting at the dock. I've located a bonanza with my partner Godfrey on the Feather River and we've established our claim. You will love this beautiful country."

Nora and her children set out on a crowded sailing vessel and a grueling six-month voyage. However, when their ship tacked into San Francisco's harbor, Andrew did not appear as promised.

Despite her devastation, Nora searched long and hard for Andrew. Legend has it that she went into the gold fields along the Feather River. Prospectors along the way knew Andrew and Godfrey. One such prospector told Nora, "They struck a pocket of gold in the streambed. Godfrey worked alone after that. He told me Andy was sick and most likely wouldn't work no more. I have my suspicions that Godfrey did away with Andy, so's he could keep the gold to hisself."

Sadly, Nora turned back to San Francisco, convinced that Andrew had been murdered. She determined that she and her children would have to fend for themselves in this new land.

Nora sold the remaining linens she had brought from Australia and bought a boardinghouse. Young Norah (named for her mother) and Sarah (Angela's future mother) took work as domestics in a nearby hotel to help support the family. Eventually, the girls found their literacy worth a whole lot more than the sweat of their brows. They opened a private school and charged a dollar a month for teaching children to read and write.

Early in the 1860s, a new road to riches, paved with silver, opened on the eastern slopes of the Sierras. Like other young, adventurous Californians, the O'Higgins girls kept an eye on developments in the Territory of Nevada, where schoolteacher pay ranged upwards of fifteen dollars a month in mining camps. In the fall of 1862, they applied for positions in the Virginia City school and gained employment. Sarah and Norah knew they would have their pick of the eligible male population in Virginia City, but to their mother they said, "Of course, we wouldn't dream of considering the 'crime' of marriage. That would mean an end to our teaching careers."

After the Northern Pacific train ride to Sacramento, tiny Sarah with large gray eyes and black curly hair and her statuesque, handsome sister, Norah, boarded a stage. It was one of those Concord-type affairs with the driver's seat on top, along with extra seats for passenger or luggage overflow.

A beefy German man wedged himself into the only remaining seat opposite the girls. As the six-horse team got under way, the man lurched forward, almost into their laps. It became harder and harder for him to maintain an upright position as he sipped from his silver flask. With the coach's canvas side curtains rolled down against the morning chill, the air inside soon became polluted with the drunk's fetid breath.

At the Truckee stage stop, the girls approached the driver with a desperate request. "Could we sit outside with you? That drunken man is fouling the air inside the coach, and if we stay there, we will surely become ill."

The stage driver responded, "As much as I'd like to have you two sweet young ladies sit with me, it's against the law. We'll just switch it around and have the German man sit with me instead."

The drunken man was none too pleased with this new seating arrangement, and the poor driver had his hands full. The only approach to ascending the winding Geigor Grade into Virginia City, crowded with freighters, was to whip the team into frenetic speed so as not to lose momentum for the next steep rise. At the most dangerous part of the road, alongside a precipitous canyon, the drunken man let out an earsplitting yell. The horses bolted, and the stage overturned and rolled partway into the canyon.

The 300-pound drunken man, the only passenger not injured in this tragedy, is said to have landed on top of Sarah's four-and-a-half-foot body. Angela described the accident:

> **Norah was literally scalped, but with great presence of mind, she replaced her own bloody scalp, fastened it down with her scarf, and went about helping the injured passengers. The driver summoned Norah to come help him "Get that bawling hunk of meat off'n that tiny girl."**
>
> **A courier was sent post haste to Virginia City for help. A doctor and stretcher-bearers took Sarah to the hospital. After examining Norah's head, Dr. Brunson pronounced her own first aid had done the work as well as any doctor could. It healed in a few days and Norah took charge of her school, but Sarah was hospitalized for nearly two years.**

When Sarah Higgins and William Tallentyre Hutchinson exchanged vows, William's future looked extremely promising. He had studied marine engineering and had been licensed by the Office of Steam Vessels. Instead of applying his skills on oceangoing steamships, he became a specialist in the building and maintenance of stamp mills that were used at ore reduction works and concentrators in the mining industry. These mechanisms, similar to giant rising and falling pestles, crushed the ore so that the minerals could be extracted.

Angela indicated that her mother and father had a stormy relationship:

**Mother was from an Irish-Catholic family and Father was English Protestant. Mother was terribly anti-British because South Ireland had been denied home rule for so many years. Father was not so devoutly anti-Catholic that he permitted religion to interfere with his family life. It was a strange combination where the blood clashed, but the yen for pioneering surmounted all conflicts.**

One swift peek at William's background explains why Sarah and William's "blood clashed." William's mother came from a family of loyal English patriots. Her grandfather, a surgeon on one of Nelson's flagships, received a shot in his heel as he climbed the rigging to restore the British flag during the Battle of Trafalgar.

William's family had lived in Alabama and Georgia before coming West to settle in California's San Joaquin Valley, bringing with them two slaves who refused to take their freedom after the Civil War. Sarah, an abolitionist, was appalled.

## The Tragedy in Virginia City

Most of the children living near the Hutchinsons' home had fathers and brothers who worked in the mines. Underground fires, scalding water, malfunctioning hoisting mechanisms, explosions, and cave-ins were considered nothing more than occupational hazards, an accepted part of the miner's life.

Katie and Jimmy Fogerty's father had just been killed in an accident. After the funeral, Joey (Angela's eleven-year-old brother and the only boy in the family) went with Katie and Jimmy to find wildflowers to put on the grave. On the way home, Jimmy and Joey decided to cool off in a nearby pond while Katie waited on the bank.

Later in the day, Katie knocked on the door of the Iowa House. When Sarah answered, the girl handed her a bundle. "Here, Mrs. Hutchinson. Here's Joey's clothes."

"Why, where's Joey?" Sarah asked.

"He's at the bottom of the pond!" Katie sobbed. "I helped Jimmy out with a stick, but Joey sank to the bottom."

Angie said the shock was so great that her mother's hair turned white overnight.

An item from the June 9, 1878, *Territorial Enterprise* tells the story of Joey's drowning.

A Boy Drowns.—Last evening about 4:30 o'clock, Joseph Penny, son of W.T. Hutchinson, Superintendent of the Iowa Mine, was drowned in a bathing place constructed by some boys in Spanish Ravine, above the mouth of Cole tunnel, in the northwestern part of the town. The boy was eleven years and nine months old and was a very bright and intelligent little fellow. There are five girls in the family and this boy was the only son. The hole in which the lad drowned was only about five feet deep. This deep part was out in the middle of the reservoir and the descent into it was sudden—off the edge of a sort of reef or ledge. Thus the boy found himself floundering beyond his depth before he knew of the danger. A boy named Fogerty, son of James Fogerty, who lost his life in the Gould and Curry mine a few days ago, came near being drowned while vainly endeavoring to save the life of young Hutchinson. Although it was known that the boys had built a dam across the ravine and made a small reservoir in which they had the habit of bathing, no one thought of the place being so deep as to be dangerous. They had a swimming pond at the same place last year but no accident ever occurred to alarm the parents of the boys frequenting the place.

After the accident, Angie's nights were filled with dreams of Joey. In an attempt to bring comfort to her grief-stricken mother, Angie recounted this dream.

**I was sitting on the end of the gold rocks dump between two large trees with an arm around the trunk of each, and the world was whirling over and over. I clung to the trees to keep from falling into space. I saw a dove fly overhead toward the hills. In telling Mama my dream, I doctored it up in a way I thought would make her happy, so I said the dove flew right down to Joey's grave. Mother attributed the dream to some spiritual power with which she thought I was endowed and that the other children did not possess. My conscience disturbed me no end about this fabrication, but I never had the heart to tell her the truth. It made me feel quite important, although, I realized I had no such psychic power.**

## The Demise of the *Santa Maria II*

The following story is from a taped interview with Monica's son, Albert Bell, before he died in 1995. He and some of his friends had been on hand when Mussolini's famous seaplane met a fiery fate on the banks of Roosevelt Lake on April 7, 1927.

Us kids used to travel up the old Fish Creek gravel road in my Model-T to fish and camp on the north side of Roosevelt Lake. On this one trip, my friends Albert Evans, the Thompson brothers, Ed Smith, Art Greer, Lloyd, and Jim came with me. [Al couldn't remember the last name of Lloyd and Jim.] We camped where the Salt River comes into Roosevelt Lake.

Airplanes were still a novelty in those days. Mussolini, the dictator of Italy, wanted to increase his prestige by being the first nation to send an airplane around the world. He built a seaplane, the *Santa Maria I*, and it flew across the Mediterranean and down the east coast of Africa, then something happened to it. So Mussolini built the *Santa Maria II*, equipped it with two big aircraft engines, and trained another crew. This seaplane flew across the Atlantic to the United States. Of course, at the time, we didn't know that the damn thing even existed.

Four of us guys went out to fish in a little rowboat with a one-cylinder outboard engine. We all smoked, but we didn't have enough money to buy cigarettes, so we'd get old butts, break out the tobacco, and roll 'em.

All of a sudden, we heard this terrific noise and saw this gigantic thing in the air right overhead. It came down low right over us with its engines roaring, and scared us death. One of the guys in our boat yelled at the pilot, "You so-and-so. You swamp us, and I'll burn you up." It was just angry talk. He didn't mean anything by it.

The seaplane landed on the water not far from us, turned around, and came up to a Standard Oil truck parked on a little road that came down to the water's edge. After filling the plane with fuel, there was some left over. One of the airmen asked all of us in little boats if we wanted the leftover gas. We only had a one-gallon can, so we didn't take any. The stupid guy then dumped the rest of the fuel into the water.

At that exact moment, one of the guys in my boat had just lit a cigarette and threw the match overboard. Instantly, the *Santa Maria II* went up in flames.

We paddled in close to the plane and began throwing water on it, but the Italians, running all around and screaming, pointed guns at us and ordered us away from the plane. We could probably have saved the *Santa Maria*, but we didn't want to get shot.

I went back to Phoenix, but the other guys stayed on at the lake. By the time I got home, the burning of the *Santa Maria* had caused a big international deal. People worried about a conspiracy. Finally, the word that some kids were responsible for the fire caught the attention of an *Arizona Republic* reporter. He went to the lake to look for us and found where the guys were camped.

This reporter cornered Wally Thompson and told him that whoever set fire to Mussolini's plane would be famous and have his picture in newspapers all over the world. Wally asked the reporter for a comb. After combing his hair, Wally proudly told the reporter, "We did it!"

Wally and his brother did end up serving time in prison but not because of this incident. The *Santa Maria*'s beautiful aircraft engines were hauled out of the lake and mounted for display in front of the courthouse in Globe.

## A Letter from Governor Hunt to Louie

GEO. W. P. HUNT
GOVERNOR

H. S. McCLUSKEY
SECRETARY

**Executive Office**
State House
Phoenix, Arizona

April 11, 1928

My dear Friend:

    One of the good citizens of your town was in to see me
today and told me that if you would offer yourself as a candidate for the Legislature that you would have clear sailing.

    I spoke to you about this some years ago, and after our
experience with the last Legislature, and the tremendous fight
that is on now to protect Arizona's sovereign right in the Colorado River, that the coming Legislature should be composed of
strong men and men who will stand up and fight for her good government. I am sure that you being a native son, would measure
up to the responsibilities and make a splendid record.

    I know you are somewhat timid and loath to enter your name
on the list, but I want you to give this your very serious consideration and run for the Legislature. Make a start. I am
sure your family, your friends in your county and yourself will
never regret your taking this step.

               Yours sincerely,

               Geo. W. P. Hunt
               Governor.

Mr. L. J. Hammer,
Casa Grande, Arizona.

## A Letter from Fred Colter

February 11, 1936

Editor of the *Messenger*

Dear Mrs. Hammer:

I am giving expression to you and the public—an intense deep feeling of gratitude and appreciation for the moral and financial aid you have given personally through publicity in your *Messenger*, your sons job printing plant and staff to myself in the past fifteen years in leading the winning fight to protect and develop Arizona's only water resources, the Colorado River.

So many times during this long and torturous firing line fight, when in extreme periods of weariness and distress brought about by opposition at home and abroad, your inspiring, encouraging, and remarkably understanding editorials were a source of renewed life to fight through their fire.

It must be ever a source of much consolation to you when three U.S. Supreme Court winning decisions in which Arizona was involved backed up our stand with other U.S. Supreme Court decisions; besides fifteen years of time showing how unworkable and vicious the Santa Fe Compact was—in fact—any state water compact.

Even President Roosevelt's National Water Resource Committee in large document official report of December, which I have just received, discussed in some detail the Colorado River Santa Fe Compact (chapter 7, pages 53 to 76 inclusive) expressing especially how unworkable this compact [would be] even when carried out in good faith.

But the Colorado River Santa Fe Compact would have been Arizona's death warrant had she signed or agreed to it either in or out of court. And would have [words undecipherable] to prevent the basic water laws that have held civilization together for thousands of years, the base and object of our Federal Constitution; annihilate our water laws, and endanger our national defense; destroy proper river planning and development of the Colorado River of which Arizona is body and backbone, and disintegrate Arizona.

I assure you it will always be an inspiration to me and should be to the people of Arizona, the part you have taken in behalf of Arizona, and I shall always, regardless of obstacles or enticement, cooperate with you to that end.

Yours faithfully

Fred T. Colter

Arizona Water Trustee

# Bibliography

Anderson, Dorothy Daniels. *Arizona Legends and Lore: Tales of Southwestern Pioneers*. Phoenix: Golden West Publishers, 1990.

Arizona Business and Professional Women's Foundation. *Women Who Made a Difference: The History of the Arizona Foundation of the Business and Professional Women*. Phoenix, 1998.

*Arizona Messenger*, 1926–1935. Microfilm. Arizona State Archives, Phoenix.

Arlington National Cemetery. *General W.S. Rosecrans*. Accessed June 2000. http://www.arlingtoncemetery.com

August, Jack L., Jr. *Vision in the Desert: Carl Hayden and Hydropolitics in the American Southwest*. Fort Worth: Texas Christian University Press, 1999.

Avery, Ben. "Picket Post: Ghost of a Ghost Town," *Arizona Highways* (April 1997): 36–38.

Barnes, Will C. *Arizona Place Names*. Tucson: University of Arizona Press, 1973.

Bell, Albert. Interview, September 1995, San Diego.

Botts, Gene, with John and Marge Osborne. *The Vulture: Gold Mine of the Century*. Phoenix: Quest Publishing Group, 1996.

Burden, Sophie. "What's Cookin'? Life and Times in Wickenburg, Arizona, 1925–1988." Manuscript prepared by Mona McCroskey from newspaper columns in the *Wickenburg Sun*.

Butruille, Susan G. *Women's Voices from the Western Frontier*. Boise, Idaho: Tamarack Books, 1995.

California Census, 1860 (film #803056). Family History Center, Mesa, Arizona.

Canty, J. Michael, and Michael N. Greeley. *History of Mining in Arizona*, vol. 2. Tucson: Mining Club of the Southwest Foundation and American Institute of Mining Engineers, 1991.

*Casa Grande Bulletin*, 1913–1917. Microfilm. Arizona State Archives, Phoenix.

*Casa Grande Dispatch*, 1914–1934. Microfilm. Arizona State Archives, Phoenix.

*Casa Grande Times*, 1912–1913. Microfilm. Arizona State Archives, Phoenix.

Clemensen, Berle A. *Casa Grande Ruins National Monument, Arizona: A Centennial History of the First Prehistoric Reserve 1892–1992*. U.S. Department of the Interior National Park Service, 1992.

Colorado Mountain History Collection. Records search by Nancy Manley, 2000. Lake County Public Library, Leadville.

Coon, Margaret. Handwritten notes compiled from old newspaper articles about guest ranches in the Wickenburg area. Wickenburg Public Library.

Dary, David. *Red Blood and Black Ink: Journalism in the Old West*. New York: Albert A. Knopf, 1998.

Egerton, Kearney. *Somewhere Out There: Arizona's Lost Mines and Vanished Treasures*. Glendale, Ariz.: Prickley Pear Press, 1974.

Goodson, Mary Rose. *The Story of Congress: Arizona's Premier Gold Camp*. Stickney, S.Dak.: Argus Publishing, 1995.

Hammer, Angela H. Diaries, 1944–1951. In the possession of the author.

———. Bert Fireman Collection. Arizona State University Archives, Tempe.

———. Hammer Papers. Arizona Collection, University of Arizona, Tucson.

Hammer, Betty Lou. Genealogy study. Phoenix, 1980.

Hammer, Mary Alice. Interview, April 2001, Phoenix.

Heathcotte, Toby, and Betty Hammer Joy. Unpublished screenplay, *Birth of the Dispatch*, based on the memoirs of Angela Hutchinson Hammer, c. 2003.

Homestead National Monument. *The Homestead Act*. Accessed June 2001. http://www.nps.gov/home/homestead_act.html

Jackson, Turrentine W. *Treasure Hill: Portrait of a Silver Mining Camp*. Reno and Las Vegas: University of Nevada Press, 1963.

James, Ronald M. *The Roar and the Silence: A History of Virginia City and the Comstock Lode*. Reno and Las Vegas: University of Nevada Press, 1998.

Jepson, Jill. "Fighting Words: Arizona's Pioneer Newspaper Battles," *Arizona Highways* (January 1999): 18–21.

Johnson, G. Wesley, Jr. *Phoenix: Valley of the Sun*. Tulsa, Okla.: Continental Heritage Press, 1982.

Karolevitz, Robert F. *Newspapering in the Old West*. New York: Bonanza Books, 1995.

Korwin, Alan. *Wickenburg: The Ultimate Guide to the Ultimate Western Town*. Phoenix: Bloomfield Press, 1994.

Land Use History of North America: Colorado Plateau. Accessed 2003. http://www.cpluhna.nau.edu/

Lyon, William H. *Old Yellow Dog Days: Frontier Journalism in Arizona, 1859–1912*. Tucson: Arizona Historical Society, 1994.

Massey, Peter, and Jeanne Wilson. *Backcountry Adventures: Arizona*. Castle Rock, Colo.: Swagman Publishing, 2001.

McFarland, Ernest W. *Mac: The Autobiography of Ernest W. McFarland*. Privately published, 1979.

Miller, Tom. *Arizona: The Land and the People*. Tucson: University of Arizona Press, 1986.

Moulton, Candy. *The Writer's Guide to Everyday Life in the Wild West: From 1840–1900*. Cincinnati, Ohio: Writer's Digest Books, 1999.

Nutt, Francis Dorothy. *Dick Wick Hall: Stories from the Salome Sun by Arizona's Most Famous Humorist*. Flagstaff, Ariz.: Northland Press, 1980.

O'Brien, Adelaide. Interview, 1990, Phoenix.

O'Brien, Anthony. Interview, 1999, Wickenburg.

Pima-Maricopa Irrigation Project. Accessed 2002–2003. http://www.gilariver.com

Paré, Madeline Ferrin, with collaboration of Bert M. Fireman. *Arizona Pageant: A Short History of the 48th State*. Phoenix: Arizona Historical Foundation, 1965.

Potter, Samuel. *A Compend of Materia Medica, Therapeutics and Prescription Writing*. Accessed November 5, 2001. http://ftp.oit.unc.edu/herbmed/eclectic/potter_comp/anti:html

Pry, Mark E. *The Town on the Hassayampa: A History of Wickenburg, Arizona*. Wickenburg: Desert Caballeros Western Museum, 1997.

Scott, Jeanne-Marie. *Anna Purdy's Wickenburg*. Wickenburg Public Library.

———. *Notes on the Early History of Sports and Recreation in the Wickenburg Area*. Wickenburg Public Library.

Las Señoras de Socorro and Ladies Auxiliary of the Maricopa County Historical Society. *The Right Side Up Town on the Upside Down River*. Wickenburg, 1975.

Sheridan, Thomas E. *Arizona: A History*. Tucson: University of Arizona Press, 1995.

Sherman, James E., and Barbara H. Sherman. *Ghost Towns of Arizona*. Norman: University of Oklahoma Press, 1969.

Smith, Duane A. "The Vulture Mine: Arizona's Golden Mirage," *Arizona and the West* 14, no. 3 (Autumn 1972): 231–52.

Smith, Grant H. *The History of the Comstock Lode*. Reno and Las Vegas: Nevada Bureau of Mines and Geology in association with the University of Nevada Press, 1998.

Spude, Robert L., and Stanley W. Paher. *Central Arizona Ghost Towns*. Las Vegas: Nevada Publications, 1978.

Szczygiel, Rosemary. Arizona Newspaper Project. Phone conversation, May 2002, Phoenix.

*Technocracy Briefs*. Numbers 22 and 50. Seattle, Wash.: Technocracy Press.

*Territorial Enterprise*, June 9, 1879. Microfilm. Nevada Historical Society Library, Reno.

Theobold, John, and Lillian Theobold, edited by Bert Fireman. *Wells Fargo in Arizona Territory*. Tempe: Arizona Historical Foundation, 1978.

Trimble, Marshall. *Arizoniana: Stories of Old Arizona Days*. Scottsdale: Reata Publishing, 1988.

Walker, Kathleen. "The Way the West Was Worn," *Arizona Highways* (October 1997): 34–37.

White, Donald. Interview, 2003, Vulture Mine.

Zarbin, Earl. *All the Time a Newspaper: The First 100 Years of the Arizona Republic*. Phoenix Newspapers, 1990.

# Index

*Note*: Italicized page numbers indicate illustrations.

# About the Author

Betty Evangeline Hammer Joy, Angela Hammer's granddaughter, grew up in Casa Grande, Arizona, where her father, Louie, operated an automotive garage and parts business. Angela became a caretaker for Betty and her brother Don Hammer after the death of their mother in 1937. After receiving her B.A. and M.A. in education at Arizona State University, Betty lived on a ranch near Bullhead City, raised five children, and later designed curriculum and taught in some of Phoenix's inner-city high schools. She now lives in the foothills of the Mingus Mountain Range in Dewey, Arizona.